The Whole-School Audit

Development Planning
for Primary and Special Schools

Brian Drakeford

School
Audit year
Headteacher
Chair of governors

David Fulton Publishers
London

David Fulton Publishers Ltd
The Chiswick Centre, 414 Chiswick High Road, London W4 5TF
www.fultonpublishers.co.uk

First published in Great Britain in 1997 by David Fulton Publishers

Note: The rights of Brian Drakeford to be identified as the authors of this work have been asserted by them in accordance with the Copyright, Designs and Patents Act 1988.

David Fulton Publishers is a division of Granada Learning Limited, part of Granada plc.

Copyright © Brian Drakeford 1997

British Library Cataloguing in Publication Data
A catalogue record for this book is available from the British Library.

ISBN 1-85346-501-1

Pages from this book may be photocopied for use only in purchasing institution. Otherwise, all rights reserved. No part of this publication may be reproduced, stored in a retieval system or transmitted, in any form or by any means, electronic, mechanical, photocopying, or otherwise, without the prior permission of the publishers.

Typeset by Brian Drakeford and Sheila Knight
Printed and bound in Great Britain

Contents

Introduction	v
National comparisons and evidence of pupil progress	1
Attitudes, behaviour and personal development	4
Attendance	9
Teaching	12
Curriculum planning – general issues	17
Curriculum planning – medium-term	21
Curriculum planning – short-term	23
The school development plan	26
Professional issues	30
Curriculum	33
Assessment, recording and reporting	37
Health education	41
Spiritual, moral, social and cultural development	44
Collective worship and assemblies	48
Support, guidance, pupils' welfare and child protection	51
Health and safety	55
Partnership with parents and the community	58
Leadership and management	62

Equal opportunities	67
Special educational needs	70
Staffing and professional development	74
Accommodation	78
Learning resources	81
School libraries	84
The efficiency of the school	87
Financial administration: additional points	91
Evaluating value for money and efficiency	95
Your school profile	98
When the Registered Inspector calls	101

Introduction

The Education Reform Act of 1988 introduced into schools in England and Wales a range of major reforms, including the National Curriculum, the transfer of certain key powers and responsibilities from LEAs to schools and new and altogether more comprehensive procedures for the monitoring of school performance.

In 1992 the Office for Standards in Education (OFSTED) was created specifically to appraise the quality and standards of education in schools and for this task explicit criteria and standardised procedures for the inspection of schools were introduced and detailed in the *Handbook for the Inspection of Schools*. According to OFSTED, such criteria and procedures are intended to promote school improvement by identifying priorities for action and to inform parents and the local community about a school's strengths and weaknesses with an emphasis on objective judgements and evaluation.[1]

In 1996 changes were made to the Framework placing a greater emphasis on a school's ability to monitor and evaluate progress towards its priorities and targets and to manage and review its own development processes. Schools are now expected to 'seek to improve (their) effectiveness, taking into account the impact of any quality assurance measures adopted.'[2]

Offering a view as to whether or not the OFSTED inspection process will actually secure 'improvement through inspection' is not the purpose of this publication. *The Whole-School Audit* has been produced in response to OFSTED's explicit inspection criteria which provide schools in England and Wales, for the first time in their history, with clear direction and standards against which they can continuously judge current strengths and weaknesses and review developmental targets.

A regular cycle of school inspections invites schools to measure up to the OFSTED criteria in their development planning. They are ill-advised to ignore the criteria until just prior to an inspection. Instead, they can adopt the OFSTED criteria as their own, plotting a course to secure sound whole-school development, a pleasing inspection report and all that follows from that happy event.

---

1 OFSTED (1995) 'New Framework for the Inspection of Schools' (Draft for consultation). OFSTED, February, p. 2.
2 OFSTED (1995) 'New Framework for the Inspection of Schools' (Draft for consultation). OFSTED, February, p. 24.

The beneficial effects of a school achieving a 'good' inspection are many and varied, including:

- enhancement of the self-esteem of staff, governors and pupils;
- improvement of the school's reputation in the area;
- maintenance of pupil numbers entering the school;
- financial stability.

This publication, then, is based on the premise that the OFSTED Inspection Framework should be regarded not as a threatening weapon to be used against schools, but as a confidence-boosting tool, facilitating regular self-review and utilised by the school for its own ends.

An OFSTED report, reviewing the inspection system itself, found that the very act of preparing for an inspection can be an effective team-building exercise for a school.[1] However, the value of pre-inspection preparation is restricted by the limited time available and the inevitable apprehension felt by all involved. By contrast, self-review over a longer period, with constant reference to the criteria, is a more powerful process, especially if it involves staff, governors, parents and pupils and actually uses the criteria in order to create policies and action for improvement.

This developmental process, arising from within the organisation itself yet keyed to the statutory framework, stands a far better chance of achieving enhanced self-confidence and commitment to change. Obvious benefits stem from the team work of all those who participate in the process. They can develop a powerful sense of ownership of their own development plan, in a way that cannot be engendered by pressure exerted on the organisation by external agencies such as OFSTED.[2]

There is an abundance of evidence to support the view that a headteacher's leadership qualities play a crucial role in the way a school's climate for change is nurtured. Hargeaves and Hopkins (1991) suggest that, for a head to be effective, he or she must be able to inspire commitment from staff and also to care passionately about the school, its members and its reputation. The same researchers have also highlighted the influence that the head's own enthusiasm has upon the change process.[3]

It is vital therefore for the head to take the lead in reviewing the school's effectiveness, since it is his or her commitment to change that will largely determine the direction in which the school moves and the pace at which it can do so. It is also for the head, working alongside governors and staff, to set the climate in which work will proceed. Hargreaves and Hopkins see the establishment of what they term *frameworks* – policies, systems and strategies – as vital in providing the structures upon which any action for change can take place. They suggest that establishing frameworks for governors, head and staff means:

- turning aims and goals into brief, written policy statements that provide consistency in interpretation and unambiguous guides to action;
- devising strategies for change and for the further development of existing policies, within which tactics may be chosen;

---

1 OFSTED (1995c) *Inspection Quality 1994/1995*. London: OFSTED
2 McLaughlin, M. (1990) 'The Rand Change Agent Study: macro perspectives and micro realities', *Educational Researcher*, **19**(9), 11–15.
3 Hargreaves, D. H. and Hopkins, D. (1991) *The Empowered School: The Management and Practice of Development Planning*. London: Cassell.

- making meetings effective by deciding on their purpose, functions, terms of reference and cycles;
- keeping permanent committees to a minimum and creating task groups with a short, fixed lease of life;
- being more effective in the management of time: to make room for new commitments, some existing activities may need to cease;
- deciding who needs to know about what and when, with appropriate channels of communication and reporting, especially on the progress of the plan;
- devising a means of judging the extent and quality of progress in development work;
- integrating the school's system for monitoring and evaluating its activities with the LEA's approach to monitoring and evaluation;
- coordinating planning cycles within the school and between the school and LEA.[1]

Working broadly along these lines, schools can use *The Whole-School Audit* to structure their work in order to secure an increasingly beneficial impact upon levels of pupil achievement. This publication will help your school to undertake an internal audit of strengths and weaknesses. It draws heavily on the statutory requirements of the Education (Schools) Act 1992, the statutory basis for the inspection of schools as detailed in the OFSTED Framework for the inspection of schools.

Its principal objective is to provide the school with a complete assessment of its current stage of development. However, for the reasons outlined earlier, the publication should not be regarded as a survival guide but rather as a means of creating, an excellent establishment which will measure up in every way to OFSTED's requirements, offering the best possible education to all its pupils.

The book's structure involves a series of audit statements, enabling staff and governors to assess:

- the quality of education provided by the school;
- the educational standards achieved by pupils;
- the efficiency with which financial resources made available to the school are managed;
- the spiritual, moral, social and cultural development of pupils.

Completion of each section of the audit will assist in the identification of the strengths and weaknesses of the school and of clear action points, leading to the compilation of an effective development plan. As the audit proceeds, those involved will encounter the principles on which OFSTED inspections are based. It is advisable to undertake the audit in conjunction with both the requirements of the OFSTED Framework and the school's development plan.

Arriving at an honest evaluation and a consensus view will inevitably give rise to valuable discussion among members of the team and enhance the professional development of all concerned. The mixing of staff and governors in the various audit teams will bring additional advantages to the school.

---

[1] Hargreaves, D. H. and Hopkins, D. (1991) *The Empowered School: The Management and Practice of Development Planning*. London: Cassell, pp. 24–25.

In setting a suitable time-scale, it would be advisable and prudent for the school to relate this to its current stage of development. Similarly, the pace at which a school can proceed effectively through the audit, and then move on into the change process, must be a matter for the individual school to decide upon.

Brian Drakeford
Lund
April, 1997

School: Audit year:

National comparisons and evidence of pupil progress

NOTES

National comparisons
The primary objective of this section of the audit is to discover what pupils know and understand and how they are progressing. In order to accomplish this task, the auditors must gather the relevant evidence required to compare the attainments of the pupils in the school with those of pupils in similar schools nationally. The key issue here is whether the attainment of pupils at 7 and 11 meets or exceeds national standards, particularly in English, mathematics and science.

The auditors need to assess how the attainments of pupils, at the time of the audit, relate to what is expected, on average, for each age group, using as points of reference what the National Curriculum says can reasonably be expected for each age group.

Progress
Having assessed what pupils know and understand, the audit proceeds to examine whether pupils are making sufficient progress in terms of gains in knowledge, understanding and skill.

Calling for evaluation of the progress pupils make – their gains in knowledge, understanding and skills – this task requires the auditors to be able to compare what pupils are achieving now with their prior attainment levels.

Evidence:

- Progress observed in lessons (e.g. What did pupils learn during the lesson or sequence of lessons?);
- Results of standardised tests on entry or annual test results;
- Samples of pupils' earlier work reviewed in the light of current work in order to assess progress;
- Progress made over longer periods of time (e.g. from one stage of school to the next);
- In KS1 it may be possible to refer to baseline assessments (e.g. profiles of pupils on entry to provide evidence of prior attainment);
- In KS2 reference can be made to KS1 tests and assessments.

School: **Audit year:**

National comparisons and evidence of pupil progress

Person responsible for this part of the audit:

1. We have a significant range of 'baseline data'.

   STRENGTH   WEAKNESS
   1   2   3   4   5   6   7

2. We analyse our 'baseline' and KS test data and plan on the basis of that analysis to monitor pupils' progress, set clear, quantifiable and measurable targets and levels of expectation and raise levels of attainment.

   STRENGTH   WEAKNESS
   1   2   3   4   5   6   7

3. The diagnostic and screening tests we use are capable of providing adequate guidance for staff.

   STRENGTH   WEAKNESS
   1   2   3   4   5   6   7

4. Our system of assessment, recording and reporting provides the school and parents with a detailed picture of progress made, prior attainment and targets for improvement.

   STRENGTH   WEAKNESS
   1   2   3   4   5   6   7

5. Our SEN records provide enough information to prepare adequate individual programmes.

   STRENGTH   WEAKNESS
   1   2   3   4   5   6   7

6. We discuss with pupils what they have learned and what they're going to do next.

   STRENGTH   WEAKNESS
   1   2   3   4   5   6   7

7. The attainments of our pupils compare with national standards, particularly in English, mathematics and science.

   STRENGTH   WEAKNESS
   1   2   3   4   5   6   7

8. We monitor the performance of different groups of pupils effectively e.g. different sexes or ethnic groups.

   STRENGTH   WEAKNESS
   1   2   3   4   5   6   7

9. The school is sustaining high levels of attainment or improving.

   STRENGTH   WEAKNESS
   1   2   3   4   5   6   7

10. We set appropriate and achievable targets for improvement e.g. improved key stage test scores and we monitor progress towards such targets.

    STRENGTH   WEAKNESS
    1   2   3   4   5   6   7

School: Audit year:

Rating for national comparisons and evidence of pupil progress

STRENGTH						WEAKNESS
1	2	3	4	5	6	7
7 points	6 points	5 points	4 points	3 points	2 points	1 point

☐ ☐ ☐ ☐ ☐ ☐ ☐ NUMBER OF RESPONSES

☐ ☐ ☐ ☐ ☐ ☐ ☐ POINTS PER LEVEL

TOTAL SCORE FOR THIS SECTION OF THE AUDIT ☐

TARGET 70

Principal strengths as identified by the audit

Principal weaknesses as identified by the audit

Action points for the next development plan

The materials in this publication may be photocopied for use only within the purchasing organisation.

School: Audit year:

Attitudes, behaviour and personal development

NOTES

The audit now considers pupils' attitudes, as these have a significant bearing on their attainment and progress and can be strongly influenced by what schools do. In particular, the auditors will examine pupils' perceptiveness, their willingness to listen to what others in the school have to say and their interest in views and ideas different from their own.

While undertaking this section of the audit, observations should be made with respect to the way in which pupils respond to the teaching in the school and other provisions, highlighting strengths and weaknesses, as shown by:

- their attitudes to learning;
- their behaviour, including incidence of exclusion;
- the quality of relationships in the school, including the degree of racial harmony where applicable;
- other aspects of the personal development of pupils, including their contributions to the life of the school community.

School: Audit year:

Attitudes, behaviour and personal development

Person responsible for this part of the audit:

1. The school's policy on behaviour and discipline outlines our strategies for encouraging a positive response from pupils.

STRENGTH						WEAKNESS
1	2	3	4	5	6	7

2. The first experience we provide for young children serves in developing positive attitudes to learning.

STRENGTH						WEAKNESS
1	2	3	4	5	6	7

3. Our pupils behave well in and around the school, and are courteous, trustworthy and show respect for property.

STRENGTH						WEAKNESS
1	2	3	4	5	6	7

4. Our pupils form constructive relationships easily with one another, with teachers and other adults, and work collaboratively when required.

STRENGTH						WEAKNESS
1	2	3	4	5	6	7

5. Our pupils show respect for other people's feelings, values and beliefs.

STRENGTH						WEAKNESS
1	2	3	4	5	6	7

6. Our pupils show initiative and a willingness to take responsibility.

STRENGTH						WEAKNESS
1	2	3	4	5	6	7

7. Our pupils show interest in their work and are able to sustain concentration and develop their capacity for personal study.

STRENGTH						WEAKNESS
1	2	3	4	5	6	7

8. Our pupils appear to enjoy their work.

STRENGTH						WEAKNESS
1	2	3	4	5	6	7

9. We ask our pupils what they are finding easy or difficult.

STRENGTH						WEAKNESS
1	2	3	4	5	6	7

10. Our pupils tackle new work with eagerness and confidence.

STRENGTH						WEAKNESS
1	2	3	4	5	6	7

11. Our pupils sense that their contributions in lessons are valued.

STRENGTH						WEAKNESS
1	2	3	4	5	6	7

The materials in this publication may be photocopied for use only within the purchasing organisation.

School: **Audit year:**

12. Our pupils, particularly younger children, are actively engaged in handling and exploring equipment and materials.

STRENGTH						WEAKNESS
1	2	3	4	5	6	7

13. Our pupils stay with an activity and do not flit between several.

STRENGTH						WEAKNESS
1	2	3	4	5	6	7

14. Our pupils concentrate well when listening to the teacher.

STRENGTH						WEAKNESS
1	2	3	4	5	6	7

15. Our pupils confidently generate ideas and solve problems.

STRENGTH						WEAKNESS
1	2	3	4	5	6	7

16. Our pupils persevere and complete tasks when difficulties arise.

STRENGTH						WEAKNESS
1	2	3	4	5	6	7

17. Our pupils make decisions independently to select and use relevant resources.

STRENGTH						WEAKNESS
1	2	3	4	5	6	7

18. Our pupils have a strong desire to improve their work.

STRENGTH						WEAKNESS
1	2	3	4	5	6	7

19. Our pupils have a pride in the finished product.

STRENGTH						WEAKNESS
1	2	3	4	5	6	7

20. There is evidence in our school of older pupils carrying more responsibility for the organisation of their work, taking initiatives and setting some of their own tasks, in discussion with their teachers.

STRENGTH						WEAKNESS
1	2	3	4	5	6	7

21. Our pupils relate well to one another, including those of different ethnic groups.

STRENGTH						WEAKNESS
1	2	3	4	5	6	7

22. Inappropriate behaviour, including harassment or bullying, by or towards particular groups of pupils, is not a problem here.

STRENGTH						WEAKNESS
1	2	3	4	5	6	7

23. Pupils work cooperatively together in lessons and support one another in school activities.

STRENGTH						WEAKNESS
1	2	3	4	5	6	7

School: **Audit year:**

24. There is a high level of respect between pupils and teachers and other adults in school, and our pupils are encouraged to articulate their own views and beliefs.

STRENGTH						WEAKNESS
1	2	3	4	5	6	7

25. Our pupils treat the school's and other people's property with respect.

STRENGTH						WEAKNESS
1	2	3	4	5	6	7

26. Our school prospectus and other information to parents describes the attitudes, behaviour and personal developments the school is seeking to promote.

STRENGTH						WEAKNESS
1	2	3	4	5	6	7

School: Audit year:

Rating for attitudes, behaviour and personal development

STRENGTH						WEAKNESS
1	2	3	4	5	6	7
7 points	6 points	5 points	4 points	3 points	2 points	1 point

☐ ☐ ☐ ☐ ☐ ☐ ☐   NUMBER OF RESPONSES

☐ ☐ ☐ ☐ ☐ ☐ ☐   POINTS PER LEVEL

TOTAL SCORE FOR THIS SECTION OF THE AUDIT ☐

TARGET 182

Principal strengths as identified by the audit

Principal weaknesses as identified by the audit

Action points for the next development plan

School: Audit year:

Attendance

NOTES

Evaluation here should focus on the level of pupils' attendance and its effect on attainment and progress.

Attendance of the great majority of pupils of primary school age is normally good, but the attendance of some pupils may be intermittent and for others it may be interrupted by long periods of illness or medical treatment.

The attendance for pupils under five is not a statutory requirement.

Where attendance falls below 90 per cent, attention should be paid to the causes of absence, to whether poor attendance or punctuality affects particular groups of pupils and to possible patterns of absence.

Evidence will include:

- a scrutiny of registers in order to identify any significant patterns of absence;
- observations of lessons and the recording of the total number of pupils present alongside the number on the register;
- delays or disruptions caused by lateness;
- discussion with staff and the education welfare officer in order to explore the extent to which attendance and punctuality is affecting teaching, attainment and progress.

School: **Audit year:**

Attendance

Person responsible for this part of the audit:

1. We have sound strategies for promoting school attendance and punctuality.

STRENGTH						WEAKNESS
1	2	3	4	5	6	7

2. The school is meeting the requirements for recording and reporting attendance.

STRENGTH						WEAKNESS
1	2	3	4	5	6	7

3. We have a process in place to follow up unauthorised absences effectively.

STRENGTH						WEAKNESS
1	2	3	4	5	6	7

School: Audit year:

Rating for attendance

STRENGTH						WEAKNESS	
1	2	3	4	5	6	7	
7 points	6 points	5 points	4 points	3 points	2 points	1 point	

☐ ☐ ☐ ☐ ☐ ☐ ☐ NUMBER OF RESPONSES

☐ ☐ ☐ ☐ ☐ ☐ ☐ POINTS PER LEVEL

TOTAL SCORE FOR THIS SECTION OF THE AUDIT ☐

TARGET 21

Principal strengths as identified by the audit

Principal weaknesses as identified by the audit

Action points for the next development plan

School: **Audit year:**

Teaching

NOTES

The quality of teaching has been identified by OFSTED as the major factor contributing to pupils' attainments, progress and responses. This then should be regarded as the most important section of the audit and the audit team must have the following issues in mind.

Firstly, any evaluation of the teaching must focus on the teacher who normally covers most or all of the curriculum for a given class; and secondly, the school's achievements must be placed in context with the way it is organised. Essential measures are:

- overall strengths and weaknesses in teaching each key stage and in different subject areas of learning;
- the extent to which teaching promotes the learning of all pupils, including those of exceptional ability, those experiencing learning difficulties and those for whom English is an additional language.

This section of the audit is also concerned with teachers' subject expertise, including their knowledge and understanding of the National Curriculum Subject Orders, the relevant syllabus for religious education and the areas of learning for pupils under five, where appropriate.

Most particularly, the audit attempts to identify the level of challenge in the content, activities and learning resources provided for pupils of different attainment levels. It seeks to assess the extent to which the teaching is suitably matched to the pupils' stages of learning, and then moves forward from that point.

Whatever teaching methods are used by the teachers, the crucial test of their effectiveness is the extent to which the pupils' knowledge and understanding are extended and deepened and by how much skill levels are increased. Teaching is likely to more effective when it has regard to:

- the type of curricular objectives being pursued;
- what pupils know, understand and can do and what they need to learn next.

The teacher's use of questions, probing pupils' knowledge and understanding, and challenging their thinking, is an essential element of effective teaching. Practical activities should aim to encourage pupils to think about what they are doing, what they have learned from it and what they need to do in order to improve their work. Investigation and problem solving activities should help pupils to apply and extend their learning in new contexts.

School: Audit year:

Teaching

Person responsible for this part of the audit:

1. We employ methods and organisational strategies which match curricular objectives and the needs of all pupils.

STRENGTH						WEAKNESS
1	2	3	4	5	6	7

2. We manage pupils well and achieve high standards of discipline.

STRENGTH						WEAKNESS
1	2	3	4	5	6	7

3. We use time and resources effectively so that pupils work productively and spend a high proportion of the available time on task.

STRENGTH						WEAKNESS
1	2	3	4	5	6	7

4. We assess pupils' work thoroughly and constructively, and use assessments to inform teaching.

STRENGTH						WEAKNESS
1	2	3	4	5	6	7

5. We make effective use of the specialist knowledge of the coordinators.

STRENGTH						WEAKNESS
1	2	3	4	5	6	7

6. The school is organised to deal effectively with pupils with special educational needs, including the most able.

STRENGTH						WEAKNESS
1	2	3	4	5	6	7

7. We identify successful and unsuccessful teaching methods.

STRENGTH						WEAKNESS
1	2	3	4	5	6	7

8. Our teachers are competent in teaching the content of the National Curriculum programmes of study and the RE syllabus.

STRENGTH						WEAKNESS
1	2	3	4	5	6	7

9. We are competent in planning activities and carrying them out.

STRENGTH						WEAKNESS
1	2	3	4	5	6	7

10. We are skilled in asking relevant questions and providing explanations.

STRENGTH						WEAKNESS
1	2	3	4	5	6	7

11. Our marking is perceptive and responds to pupils' work.

STRENGTH						WEAKNESS
1	2	3	4	5	6	7

The materials in this publication may be photocopied for use only within the purchasing organisation.

School: **Audit year:**

12. We draw on a range of contexts and resources to make subject knowledge comprehensible to pupils.

    STRENGTH   WEAKNESS
    1   2   3   4   5   6   7

13. We successfully provide demanding work for more able pupils.

    STRENGTH   WEAKNESS
    1   2   3   4   5   6   7

14. Our teachers set high expectations so as to challenge pupils and deepen their knowledge and understanding.

    STRENGTH   WEAKNESS
    1   2   3   4   5   6   7

15. Our teachers make clear to pupils the importance of application, accuracy and good presentation.

    STRENGTH   WEAKNESS
    1   2   3   4   5   6   7

16. Our teachers stress the need to use critical thinking, creativity and imagination.

    STRENGTH   WEAKNESS
    1   2   3   4   5   6   7

17. The work we plan provides the stimulus, the knowledge and the methods required in order for pupils to do their best.

    STRENGTH   WEAKNESS
    1   2   3   4   5   6   7

18. We are setting appropriate expectations for all pupils and providing adequate resources, support or time for them to undertake work effectively.

    STRENGTH   WEAKNESS
    1   2   3   4   5   6   7

19. Our lesson planning indicates very clearly the learning objectives and how teaching will be organised to challenge pupils.

    STRENGTH   WEAKNESS
    1   2   3   4   5   6   7

20. Continuity and progression in each subject has been considered.

    STRENGTH   WEAKNESS
    1   2   3   4   5   6   7

21. We consider how lessons fit into longer-term planning.

    STRENGTH   WEAKNESS
    1   2   3   4   5   6   7

22. Support staff are informed about teaching and learning objectives and are involved in planning.

    STRENGTH   WEAKNESS
    1   2   3   4   5   6   7

School: **Audit year:**

23. Our teachers employ methods and organisational strategies which match curricular objectives and the needs of all pupils.

STRENGTH						WEAKNESS
1	2	3	4	5	6	7

24. Our teachers manage pupils well and achieve high standards of discipline.

STRENGTH						WEAKNESS
1	2	3	4	5	6	7

25. The pace of lessons is brisk, allowing for occasions which need time for reflection and consolidation or for steady and careful pursuit of a task.

STRENGTH						WEAKNESS
1	2	3	4	5	6	7

School: **Audit year:**

Rating for teaching

STRENGTH						WEAKNESS
1	2	3	4	5	6	7
7 points	6 points	5 points	4 points	3 points	2 points	1 point

☐ ☐ ☐ ☐ ☐ ☐ ☐ NUMBER OF RESPONSES

☐ ☐ ☐ ☐ ☐ ☐ ☐ POINTS PER LEVEL

TOTAL SCORE FOR THIS SECTION OF THE AUDIT ☐

TARGET 175

Principal strengths as identified by the audit

Principal weaknesses as identified by the audit

Action points for the next development plan

School: Audit year:

Curriculum planning – general issues

NOTES

Good curriculum planning should be regarded as a means of ensuring clear objectives for what pupils are to learn and how these objectives will be achieved, taking into account the differing needs of pupils.

The key to this aspect of the audit is to form judgements as to whether the planning methods and organisational arrangements adopted by the school are fit for the purpose of achieving high standards of work and behaviour. The evidence for this must stem directly from actual lesson observation.

Auditors are advised to discuss with teachers why particular teaching methods are used as this will shed light on the way they plan and how readily they are able to respond to changing classroom situations.

Whatever the teaching methods or organisational strategies adopted by the school, the audit will assess the extent to which these are suited to the objectives of the lesson. Factors such as the number of pupils, their age, attainment and behaviour will be assessed with direct evidence arising from lesson observation and the examination of planning documents and procedures.

The planning of topic work in particular must be examined rigorously, with particular attention paid to structure and progression.

For the purpose of this audit, curriculum planning has been divided into the following sections:

- general issues, including long-term planning;
- medium-term planning;
- short-term planning.

School: **Audit year:**

Curriculum planning – general issues

Person responsible for this part of the audit:

1. Our planning covers all the areas of learning for under-fives.

STRENGTH						WEAKNESS
1	2	3	4	5	6	7

2. Our planning incorporates National Curriculum programmes of study and the requirements of the agreed syllabus for religious education and we use the revised National Curriculum to define the learning objectives against which assessments can be made.

STRENGTH						WEAKNESS
1	2	3	4	5	6	7

3. Our planning sets out clear objectives and summarises what pupils will do and the resources they will need.

STRENGTH						WEAKNESS
1	2	3	4	5	6	7

4. Our planning shows how knowledge and understanding can be extended and work adapted to suit pupils who learn at different rates.

STRENGTH						WEAKNESS
1	2	3	4	5	6	7

5. Our teachers assess pupils' work thoroughly and constructively and use assessments to inform their planning.

STRENGTH						WEAKNESS
1	2	3	4	5	6	7

6. The impact of joint planning arrangements on the quality of what is planned is good.

STRENGTH						WEAKNESS
1	2	3	4	5	6	7

7. Our planning documents are a significant component of the school's recording system.

STRENGTH						WEAKNESS
1	2	3	4	5	6	7

8. Our medium- and short-term planning documents are valuable components of the school's recording system.

STRENGTH						WEAKNESS
1	2	3	4	5	6	7

9. Our learning objectives refer to learning in terms of what pupils will know (knowledge) understand (concepts) and be able to do (skills).

STRENGTH						WEAKNESS
1	2	3	4	5	6	7

School: **Audit year:**

10. Our learning objectives define learning outcomes for pupils, NOT activities to be undertaken.

STRENGTH						WEAKNESS
1	2	3	4	5	6	7

11. In some circumstances, e.g. the arts, our learning objectives often refer to opportunities or experiences which pupils will have.

STRENGTH						WEAKNESS
1	2	3	4	5	6	7

12. Our learning objectives are as specific as possible and provide for the range of abilities and needs in a class, deriving from the programmes of study and objectives identified in medium-term planning.

STRENGTH						WEAKNESS
1	2	3	4	5	6	7

13. Where possible our learning objectives are observable, measurable and assessable and frequently begin with 'to' e.g. *To know . . . To be able to . . . To understand . . .*

STRENGTH						WEAKNESS
1	2	3	4	5	6	7

14. There is a school collection (the Schemes of Work) of guidance aimed at children of different ages and abilities.

STRENGTH						WEAKNESS
1	2	3	4	5	6	7

15. Our subject coordinators have written the guidance for their own subject throughout the school, in collaboration with colleagues and class teachers interpret the guidance provided for subjects to create a coherent curriculum.

STRENGTH						WEAKNESS
1	2	3	4	5	6	7

16. The school's governing body plays an active role in curriculum planning.

STRENGTH						WEAKNESS
1	2	3	4	5	6	7

School: **Audit year:**

Rating for curriculum planning – general issues

STRENGTH						WEAKNESS
1	2	3	4	5	6	7
7 points	6 points	5 points	4 points	3 points	2 points	1 point

☐ ☐ ☐ ☐ ☐ ☐ ☐ NUMBER OF RESPONSES

☐ ☐ ☐ ☐ ☐ ☐ ☐ POINTS PER LEVEL

TOTAL SCORE FOR THIS SECTION OF THE AUDIT ☐

TARGET 112

Principal strengths as identified by the audit

Principal weaknesses as identified by the audit

Action points for the next development plan

School: Audit year:

Curriculum planning – medium-term

Person responsible for this part of the audit:

1. Our medium-term planning serves to identify the broad learning objectives.

STRENGTH						WEAKNESS
1	2	3	4	5	6	7

2. Our medium-term plan is a compilation of the schemes of work for all subjects taught during the term or half-term.

STRENGTH						WEAKNESS
1	2	3	4	5	6	7

3. The purpose of our medium-term plan is to develop each year group plan into a detailed sequence of continuing, blocked and linked units of work.

STRENGTH						WEAKNESS
1	2	3	4	5	6	7

4. Our medium-term planning is undertaken by small groups of teachers or year group coordinators working collaboratively with the support of subject coordinators.

STRENGTH						WEAKNESS
1	2	3	4	5	6	7

5. The medium-term plan provides guidance for teachers about how to plan and implement the units of work in each subject.

STRENGTH						WEAKNESS
1	2	3	4	5	6	7

6. Our medium-term planning reflects the school's principles, aims and policies and addresses the appropriate range of ability.

STRENGTH						WEAKNESS
1	2	3	4	5	6	7

7. Our medium-term planning identifies the parts of the National Curriculum Programmes of Study and the R. E. Agreed Syllabus etc. to be covered, together with the broad learning objectives.

STRENGTH						WEAKNESS
1	2	3	4	5	6	7

8. Our medium-term planning outlines those activities which enable achievement of the learning objectives (including resource implications and time allocation).

STRENGTH						WEAKNESS
1	2	3	4	5	6	7

The materials in this publication may be photocopied for use only within the purchasing organisation.

School: **Audit year:**

Rating for curriculum planning – medium-term

STRENGTH						WEAKNESS
1	2	3	4	5	6	7
7 points	6 points	5 points	4 points	3 points	2 points	1 point
☐	☐	☐	☐	☐	☐	☐ NUMBER OF RESPONSES
☐	☐	☐	☐	☐	☐	☐ POINTS PER LEVEL

TOTAL SCORE FOR THIS SECTION OF THE AUDIT ☐

TARGET **56**

Principal strengths as identified by the audit

```
[                                                                      ]
```

Principal weaknesses as identified by the audit

```
[                                                                      ]
```

Action points for the next development plan

```
[                                                                      ]
```

School: Audit year:

Curriculum planning – short-term

Person responsible for this part of the audit:

1. Our short-term planning is derived from the medium-term plan and addresses all work to be undertaken by pupils over a short period, e.g. two weeks, one week or a day

STRENGTH						WEAKNESS
1	2	3	4	5	6	7

2. Our short-term planning uses the results of assessment to address the needs of individual pupils and as far as possible involves pupils in the process so that they begin to have ownership of their own learning.

STRENGTH						WEAKNESS
1	2	3	4	5	6	7

3. The key elements of our short-term plans are:

   learning objectives;
   learning activities, including arrangements for differentiation
   assessment and an indication of future work;
   evaluation;
   special resources;
   time allocation.

STRENGTH						WEAKNESS
1	2	3	4	5	6	7

4. In our short-term planning, the broad objectives identified in our medium-term plans are broken down into achievable specific learning objectives matching the needs of the pupils.

STRENGTH						WEAKNESS
1	2	3	4	5	6	7

5. Achievement or non-achievement of the learning objectives are recorded in our short-term planning documents and this is used to inform future planning, ensuring effective differentiation and facilitating matching to pupils' learning needs.

STRENGTH						WEAKNESS
1	2	3	4	5	6	7

6. Our short-term plans are detailed daily or weekly plans written by class teachers and appropriate records are used to ensure effective day-to-day teaching and assessment. They include suitably differentiated pupil activities based on clear learning objectives.

STRENGTH						WEAKNESS
1	2	3	4	5	6	7

School: **Audit year:**

7. Whilst being in a similar format to the medium-term plan, our short-term planning has a more precise focus for learning objectives for groups of children or individuals, and also addresses teaching strategies such as style, grouping and methods of differentiation.

STRENGTH						WEAKNESS
1	2	3	4	5	6	7

8. Our short-term planning facilitates adequate differentiation and provides a balance of different types of activity throughout the week.

STRENGTH						WEAKNESS
1	2	3	4	5	6	7

9. Our short-term planning aims provides an appropriate pace of learning and allows for monitoring, evaluating and (if required) modifying the medium-term plan.

STRENGTH						WEAKNESS
1	2	3	4	5	6	7

10. The formative and diagnostic assessments in our short-term planning are inextricably linked.

STRENGTH						WEAKNESS
1	2	3	4	5	6	7

11. Our short-term planning contains clearly defined, achievable learning objectives ensuring that formative assessment is manageable.

STRENGTH						WEAKNESS
1	2	3	4	5	6	7

12. Our learning objectives are related to the National Curriculum (when appropriate).

STRENGTH						WEAKNESS
1	2	3	4	5	6	7

13. The workload with respect to short-term planning here has been kept to the minimum necessary to achieve the required outcomes.

STRENGTH						WEAKNESS
1	2	3	4	5	6	7

The materials in this publication may be photocopied for use only within the purchasing organisation.

School: Audit year:

Rating for curriculum planning – short-term

STRENGTH						WEAKNESS
1	2	3	4	5	6	7
7 points	6 points	5 points	4 points	3 points	2 points	1 point

☐ ☐ ☐ ☐ ☐ ☐ ☐   NUMBER OF RESPONSES

☐ ☐ ☐ ☐ ☐ ☐ ☐   POINTS PER LEVEL

TOTAL SCORE FOR THIS SECTION OF THE AUDIT ☐

TARGET 91

Principal strengths as identified by the audit

Principal weaknesses as identified by the audit

Action points for the next development plan

The materials in this publication may be photocopied for use only within the purchasing organisation.

School: **Audit year:**

The school development plan

NOTES

Effective school development planning focuses on the improvement of educational outcomes and relates expenditure to that end. The school should be able to demonstrate that it budgets systematically for new and well-targeted expenditure, as distinct from merely repeating previous years' spending patterns.

An effective school development plan should provide evidence of the fact that the school is looking ahead, with detailed planning ready for the forthcoming year and outline planning for at least one or two years beyond that.

This audit attempts to identify the extent to which financial planning is based on good current data and clear projections and whether it provides strategies for managing expenditure and handling contingencies.

The audit is also concerned with whether targets specified in the *current* school development plan represent the right issues to be pursuing in relation to the school's circumstances and needs at the current time.

School development planning is likely to be most effective when it involves all staff and governors in the processes of planning, implementation and review.

School: Audit year:

The school development plan

Person responsible for this part of the audit:

1. Our School Development Plan (SDP) reflects the main findings of a whole-school audit indicating the existing situation, strengths and weaknesses.

STRENGTH						WEAKNESS
1	2	3	4	5	6	7

2. The priorities of our SDP are aligned with:

   the central aims of the school;
   the requirements of national initiatives LEA/local school cluster group policies.

STRENGTH						WEAKNESS
1	2	3	4	5	6	7

3. Our SDP makes it clear to every teacher and every member of the governing body:

   what the tasks are;
   what other people's tasks are, and who the line manager is;
   what deadline has been set for the completion of each section of the plan;
   what the available budget is and the resources available;
   why the school is attempting to achieve the targets set;
   how it can be known when targets have been achieved (*success criteria*);
   what the benefits will be in terms of pupils' learning and to the standards attained.

STRENGTH						WEAKNESS
1	2	3	4	5	6	7

4. There are clear links between the SDP and the school's management of its budget.

STRENGTH						WEAKNESS
1	2	3	4	5	6	7

5. Our SDP covers the long- and short-term intentions in an appropriate balance so that the shorter term targets are clearly charted stages in the achievement of the longer term.

STRENGTH						WEAKNESS
1	2	3	4	5	6	7

6. Our SDP is well published to all interested parties.

STRENGTH						WEAKNESS
1	2	3	4	5	6	7

7. Our SDP makes clear where help can be found for every teacher and how each teacher's professional development will be enhanced in the process of implementing the plan.

STRENGTH						WEAKNESS
1	2	3	4	5	6	7

8. We put as much time and energy into making the SDP work as we did into devising it.

STRENGTH						WEAKNESS
1	2	3	4	5	6	7

The materials in this publication may be photocopied for use only within the purchasing organisation.

School: **Audit year:**

9. We make it clear to everybody concerned who to consult and report to on each part of SDP work.

STRENGTH						WEAKNESS
1	2	3	4	5	6	7

10. Our system for reporting on progress is effective e.g. the meetings are neither too long nor too frequent.

STRENGTH						WEAKNESS
1	2	3	4	5	6	7

11. We are aware of the importance of sustaining people's motivation and confidence during the stage of making the SDP work.

STRENGTH						WEAKNESS
1	2	3	4	5	6	7

12. We have the flexibility to postpone SDP deadlines or reduce the amount of work we had aimed to cover in a given time if this is deemed necessary.

STRENGTH						WEAKNESS
1	2	3	4	5	6	7

13. We note how the SDP proceeds in order to improve the process by which the next planning phase is undertaken.

STRENGTH						WEAKNESS
1	2	3	4	5	6	7

14. The governors have a long-term view of where the school should be heading.

STRENGTH						WEAKNESS
1	2	3	4	5	6	7

15. The Staff have a long-term view of where the school should be heading.

STRENGTH						WEAKNESS
1	2	3	4	5	6	7

16. The governors take a systematic approach to the analysis of the school's current and future situation. Expectations are high and there are shared values and norms about learning, behaviour and relationships.

STRENGTH						WEAKNESS
1	2	3	4	5	6	7

17. Our staff take a systematic approach to the analysis of the school's current and future situation. Expectations are high and there are shared values and norms about learning, behaviour and relationships.

STRENGTH						WEAKNESS
1	2	3	4	5	6	7

The materials in this publication may be photocopied for use only within the purchasing organisation.

School: Audit year:

Rating for the school development plan

STRENGTH						WEAKNESS
1	2	3	4	5	6	7
7 points	6 points	5 points	4 points	3 points	2 points	1 point

☐ ☐ ☐ ☐ ☐ ☐ ☐ NUMBER OF RESPONSES

☐ ☐ ☐ ☐ ☐ ☐ ☐ POINTS PER LEVEL

TOTAL SCORE FOR THIS SECTION OF THE AUDIT ☐

TARGET 119

Principal strengths as identified by the audit

Principal weaknesses as identified by the audit

Action points for the next development plan

The materials in this publication may be photocopied for use only within the purchasing organisation.

School: Audit year:

Professional issues

NOTES

This section of the audit concentrates on the way in which plans are translated into practice and the extent to which teaching sets high expectations and promotes the learning of all pupils.

Underpinning these aspects will be the quality of guidance provided for staff in the form of professional development and INSET provision, with clear planning, documentation and procedures.

The head teacher, as the professional leader of the school, has direct responsibility for the sustained improvement of quality and standards, for ensuring equality of opportunity for all pupils and for the development of policies and the deployment of resources to achieve these ends.

The staff development and INSET programme should effectively motivate staff by identifying and meeting individual and corporate needs. Programmes of professional development should contribute positively and directly to the quality of teaching.

Forms of evidence should include:

- observation of lessons;
- scrutiny of pupils' work and how it is marked;
- discussion with teachers and support staff.

School: Audit year:

Professional issues

Person responsible for this part of the audit:

1. Our staff handbook includes a policy for professional development and INSET provision.

STRENGTH						WEAKNESS
1	2	3	4	5	6	7

2. Our schemes of work and teachers' planning documents provide insights into teaching methods, INSET programme and organisational strategies deployed in the school, and their relationship with the sequence of work and curricular objectives.

STRENGTH						WEAKNESS
1	2	3	4	5	6	7

3. We have all necessary documents in place in preparation for an OFSTED inspection (see page 84).

STRENGTH						WEAKNESS
1	2	3	4	5	6	7

4. We have devised clear programmes of action and we target resources, particularly staff time and funding for curriculum and staff development, to manage the implementation within the time intended.

STRENGTH						WEAKNESS
1	2	3	4	5	6	7

The materials in this publication may be photocopied for use only within the purchasing organisation.

School: **Audit year:**

Rating for professional issues

STRENGTH						WEAKNESS
1	2	3	4	5	6	7
7 points	6 points	5 points	4 points	3 points	2 points	1 point

☐ ☐ ☐ ☐ ☐ ☐ ☐ NUMBER OF RESPONSES

☐ ☐ ☐ ☐ ☐ ☐ ☐ POINTS PER LEVEL

TOTAL SCORE FOR THIS SECTION OF THE AUDIT ☐

TARGET 28

Principal strengths as identified by the audit

Principal weaknesses as identified by the audit

Action points for the next development plan

School: Audit year:

Curriculum

NOTES

This section focuses on the planning and content of the curriculum and its contribution to the educational standards achieved by all pupils, taking into account their age, capability, gender, ethnicity, background and special educational needs.

Judgements concerning the extent to which the curriculum meets the needs of all pupils should be focused on what is taught rather than what is documented. Central to all other considerations in this section of the audit is the question of whether the curriculum provided by the school meets the statutory requirements of the National Curriculum, including religious education and sex education, where these apply. Providing these statutory requirements are being met, it is for the school to determine the character of its curriculum and the mode of its delivery.

Forms of evidence include:

- the school's curriculum policy guidelines and schemes of work;
- comparison of curriculum plans and practice by means of the observation of lessons, including shadowing individual pupil's experience of the curriculum;
- analysis and observation of extra-curricular activities for all pupils;
- scrutiny of samples of pupils' work and records, including National Curriculum assessment;
- discussion with teachers, support staff and pupils and concentrating on how curriculum organisation is affecting pupils' attainments and progress;
- examination of individual education plans, statements and annual reviews to establish the appropriateness of provision for pupils with special educational needs.

School: Audit year:

Curriculum

Person responsible for this part of the audit:

1. Our curriculum meets the statutory requirements to teach the subjects of the National Curriculum, and religious education.

STRENGTH						WEAKNESS
1	2	3	4	5	6	7

2. In English, we have evidence with regards to the contribution made by other subjects to pupils' competence in reading, writing, speaking and listening.

STRENGTH						WEAKNESS
1	2	3	4	5	6	7

3. In mathematics, we have evidence of the use of number in other subjects.

STRENGTH						WEAKNESS
1	2	3	4	5	6	7

4. We have evidence of the use of information technology in other subject areas.

STRENGTH						WEAKNESS
1	2	3	4	5	6	7

5. Our curriculum provides equality of access and opportunity for pupils to make progress.

STRENGTH						WEAKNESS
1	2	3	4	5	6	7

6. Our curriculum meets the requirements of all pupils on the school's Code of Practice special educational needs register.

STRENGTH						WEAKNESS
1	2	3	4	5	6	7

7. Our curriculum is enriched by extra-curricular provision, including sport.

STRENGTH						WEAKNESS
1	2	3	4	5	6	7

8. There is clear evidence of the programmes of study in our classroom work.

STRENGTH						WEAKNESS
1	2	3	4	5	6	7

9. Adequate time has been made available for teaching the different components of the curriculum.

STRENGTH						WEAKNESS
1	2	3	4	5	6	7

10. Our pupils are able to cover the required material in appropriate depth.

STRENGTH						WEAKNESS
1	2	3	4	5	6	7

School: **Audit year:**

11. Our curriculum organisation facilitates the selection of material from earlier or later key stages enabling pupils to progress at their own pace and demonstrate achievement.

STRENGTH						WEAKNESS
1	2	3	4	5	6	7

12. There is whole-school agreement about subject coverage and the balance between subjects and topics.

STRENGTH						WEAKNESS
1	2	3	4	5	6	7

13. Curriculum outcomes are being monitored by senior staff and there is a system in place to monitor whether there is adequate consistency of work between classes.

STRENGTH						WEAKNESS
1	2	3	4	5	6	7

14. Reference is made in our curriculum planning not only to the knowledge, understanding and skills which teachers expect pupils to develop, but also to the teaching methods and organisational strategies to be employed to achieve these goals.

STRENGTH						WEAKNESS
1	2	3	4	5	6	7

School: **Audit year:**

Rating for curriculum

STRENGTH						WEAKNESS
1	2	3	4	5	6	7
7 points	6 points	5 points	4 points	3 points	2 points	1 point

☐ ☐ ☐ ☐ ☐ ☐ ☐ NUMBER OF RESPONSES

☐ ☐ ☐ ☐ ☐ ☐ ☐ POINTS PER LEVEL

TOTAL SCORE FOR THIS SECTION OF THE AUDIT ☐

TARGET 98

Principal strengths as identified by the audit

```
```

Principal weaknesses as identified by the audit

```
```

Action points for the next development plan

```
```

School: Audit year:

Assessment, recording and reporting

NOTES

First and foremost, pupil assessment should be accurate and used in the planning of future work. Particular attention should be given to the use of assessment data in responding to the needs of individual pupils.

A review of documentation, together with discussion with teachers, will provide a context for observing classroom assessment. Teachers' assessments should relate accurately to National Curriculum requirements where these apply. However, teachers are not required to maintain detailed records: they need only collect samples of work which exemplify attainment at each level.

The degree of transferability of pupil records, as pupils move through the school, should be carefully considered while undertaking this section of the audit.

Examples of evidence are:

- comparison of pupils' work with teachers' assessments and records;
- samples of work and assessments which test the comparability of individual teachers' judgements.

School: **Audit year:**

Assessment, recording and reporting

Person responsible for this part of the audit:

1. Our system of ARR is manageable, integrating curriculum planning, assessment, recording and reporting so that each process is not an additional burden for our staff.

   STRENGTH   WEAKNESS
   1   2   3   4   5   6   7

2. There are effective systems for assessing pupils' attainments in place.

   STRENGTH   WEAKNESS
   1   2   3   4   5   6   7

3. Assessment information is used to inform curriculum planning.

   STRENGTH   WEAKNESS
   1   2   3   4   5   6   7

4. Our teachers' assessments relate accurately to both National Curriculum requirements and external validation arrangements, where these apply.

   STRENGTH   WEAKNESS
   1   2   3   4   5   6   7

5. We are collecting samples of work which exemplify attainment at each level.

   STRENGTH   WEAKNESS
   1   2   3   4   5   6   7

6. We keep formal educational records on every pupil, including material on academic achievements, other skills and abilities and progress in school.

   STRENGTH   WEAKNESS
   1   2   3   4   5   6   7

7. These summaries are concise and informative and used to inform reports.

   STRENGTH   WEAKNESS
   1   2   3   4   5   6   7

8. We update these records at least once a year.

   STRENGTH   WEAKNESS
   1   2   3   4   5   6   7

9. We give our parents access to these records.

   STRENGTH   WEAKNESS
   1   2   3   4   5   6   7

10. Whenever a pupil moves to another school, his/her records are transferred to the receiving school within 15 school days of that pupil ceasing to be registered here or within 15 school days of the new school requesting the records.

    STRENGTH   WEAKNESS
    1   2   3   4   5   6   7

School: **Audit year:**

11. The school has a prospectus showing, at least in outline, how far the school's planned curriculum meets statutory requirements.

STRENGTH						WEAKNESS
1	2	3	4	5	6	7

12. We keep abilities and progress in school records on every child, including information on academic achievements, other skills and progress in school.

STRENGTH						WEAKNESS
1	2	3	4	5	6	7

13. We avoid writing information twice.

STRENGTH						WEAKNESS
1	2	3	4	5	6	7

14. Up-to-date information about any individual pupil can be accessed easily.

STRENGTH						WEAKNESS
1	2	3	4	5	6	7

15. We recognise that pupil records have a key role in ensuring that information on pupils' performance is transferred and used as they move through the school.

STRENGTH						WEAKNESS
1	2	3	4	5	6	7

16. We have established sound procedures for monitoring and evaluating the outcomes of work, including the use of quantitative data where appropriate, in order to judge the extent to which priorities are achieved.

STRENGTH						WEAKNESS
1	2	3	4	5	6	7

School: Audit year:

Rating for assessment, recording and reporting

STRENGTH						WEAKNESS
1	2	3	4	5	6	7
7 points	6 points	5 points	4 points	3 points	2 points	1 point

☐ ☐ ☐ ☐ ☐ ☐ ☐   NUMBER OF RESPONSES

☐ ☐ ☐ ☐ ☐ ☐ ☐   POINTS PER LEVEL

TOTAL SCORE FOR THIS SECTION OF THE AUDIT ☐

TARGET 112

Principal strengths as identified by the audit

Principal weaknesses as identified by the audit

Action points for the next development plan

School: Audit year:

Health education

NOTES

Health education is an important agent in the school for promoting physical, social and mental well-being of pupils. This section of the audit examines the extent to which important aspects of health education can be observed in subject work and in the daily routines of the school.

Governing bodies are required to have a policy with respect to sex education, although schools are not required to provide it. Schools should also have clear policies concerning the dangers of drug misuse.

Examples of evidence include:

- pupils' knowledge and understanding of health issues;
- pupils' awareness of their ability to make choices relating to their health.

School: Audit year:

Health education

Person responsible for this part of the audit:

1. Our policy for drugs education aims to give pupils the facts, emphasising the benefits of a healthy lifestyle, and gives them the knowledge and skills to make informed and healthy choices now and later in life.

   STRENGTH   WEAKNESS
      1   2   3   4   5   6   7

2. We have clear policies and procedures for dealing with drug-related incidents on the school premises and for working with other services offering young people appropriate support and advice.

   STRENGTH   WEAKNESS
      1   2   3   4   5   6   7

3. The governing body has a policy on whether or not to provide sex education.

   STRENGTH   WEAKNESS
      1   2   3   4   5   6   7

4. Our parents have been consulted and informed about the policy for sex education.

   STRENGTH   WEAKNESS
      1   2   3   4   5   6   7

5. Parents have been informed about their right to withdraw their children from some elements of any sex education programme.

   STRENGTH   WEAKNESS
      1   2   3   4   5   6   7

6. Our provision for health education is planned, coherent and appropriate to the ages and needs of pupils.

   STRENGTH   WEAKNESS
      1   2   3   4   5   6   7

7. Our pupils have a sound knowledge and understanding of health issues and an awareness of their ability to make choices relating to their health.

   STRENGTH   WEAKNESS
      1   2   3   4   5   6   7

School: Audit year:

Health education

STRENGTH						WEAKNESS
1	2	3	4	5	6	7
7 points	6 points	5 points	4 points	3 points	2 points	1 point

☐ ☐ ☐ ☐ ☐ ☐ ☐ NUMBER OF RESPONSES

☐ ☐ ☐ ☐ ☐ ☐ ☐ POINTS PER LEVEL

TOTAL SCORE FOR THIS SECTION OF THE AUDIT ☐

TARGET 49

Principal strengths as identified by the audit

Principal weaknesses as identified by the audit

Action points for the next development plan

The materials in this publication may be photocopied for use only within the purchasing organisation.

School: **Audit year:**

Spiritual, moral, social and cultural development

NOTES

The class teacher's responsibility for all aspects of the curriculum facilitates a coherent approach to spiritual, moral, social, cultural and intellectual development. This aspect of the audit helps to evaluate the extent to which provision reaches all pupils, whatever their backgrounds.

Spiritual development
Effective provision for spiritual development depends on there being a curriculum in place having appropriate approaches to teaching and embodying clear values. With such a provision pupils gain understanding through reflection on their own and other peoples' lives and beliefs, and their environment. This relies on teachers receiving and valuing pupils' ideas across the whole curriculum and acts of worship can play a particular part here. While religious education and spiritual development are not synonymous, religious education can make a significant contribution to spiritual development.

Moral development
The audit attempts to assess the extent to which the school has an established framework of values regulating personal behaviour through principles, rather than through fear of punishment or by means of rewards. These principles should foster values such as honesty, fairness and respect for truth and justice.

Social development
Social development in schools is dependent on the acceptance of group rules and an ability to set oneself in a wider context. The quality of relationships in schools is a vital factor in the learning process by which pupils' attitudes to good social behaviour and self-discipline are formed.

Cultural development
Cultural development is concerned with participation in and the appreciation of cultural activities and tradition. The audit seeks to assess how the school widens its pupils' knowledge and experience of their own and other cultural traditions.
  Examples of evidence include:

- observation of lessons and daily routines in and around the school, collective worship and assemblies, extra-curricular activities;
- examination of the agreed syllabus for religious education, curriculum guidelines and schemes of work;
- assessment of the range and quality of resources used to bring pupils into contact with different aspects of social and cultural traditions;
- observation of pupil responsibilities around the school and opportunities for pupils' own initiatives;
- discussion with teachers and other staff of the moral values promoted by the school;
- observation to establish whether pupils are treated consistently.

School: **Audit year:**

Spiritual, moral, social and cultural development

Person responsible for this part of the audit:

1. We provide our pupils with knowledge and insight into values and beliefs enabling them to reflect on their experiences in a way which develops their spiritual awareness and self-knowledge.

STRENGTH						WEAKNESS
1	2	3	4	5	6	7

2. We teach the principles which distinguish right from wrong.

STRENGTH						WEAKNESS
1	2	3	4	5	6	7

3. We encourage pupils to relate positively to others, take responsibility, participate fully in the community, and develop an understanding of citizenship.

STRENGTH						WEAKNESS
1	2	3	4	5	6	7

4. We teach pupils to appreciate their own cultural traditions and the diversity and richness of other cultures.

STRENGTH						WEAKNESS
1	2	3	4	5	6	7

5. We use our curriculum as a vehicle for promoting personal development in all its forms.

STRENGTH						WEAKNESS
1	2	3	4	5	6	7

6. The school provides its pupils with knowledge and insight into values and religious beliefs and enables them to reflect on their experiences in a way which develops their self-knowledge and spiritual awareness.

STRENGTH						WEAKNESS
1	2	3	4	5	6	7

7. The school provides a moral code as a basis for behaviour which is promoted through the life of the school.

STRENGTH						WEAKNESS
1	2	3	4	5	6	7

8. We look at the opportunities for pupils to develop and express moral values and extend social and personal understanding across a range of issues, including, for example, personal rights and responsibilities and equal opportunities.

STRENGTH						WEAKNESS
1	2	3	4	5	6	7

9. We encourage pupils to explore ideas about such issues in all areas of the curriculum via well-chosen stories and sensitive discussion of incidents that arise in school or outside. This discussion is also used to help children distinguish right from wrong behaviour.

STRENGTH						WEAKNESS
1	2	3	4	5	6	7

The materials in this publication may be photocopied for use only within the purchasing organisation.

School: **Audit year:**

10. We use aspects of the curriculum such as history, geography, art, music, dance, drama and literature to make positive contributions, for example, through opportunities for pupils to:

    visit museums and art galleries;
    work with artists, authors and performers;
    develop openness towards and value the music and dance of different cultures;
    appreciate the natural world through art and literature;
    recognise the contribution of many cultures to mathematics and to scientific and technological development.

STRENGTH						WEAKNESS
1	2	3	4	5	6	7

11. Our school prospectus, curricular documentation, staff handbook and code of behaviour give a preliminary view of how the school seeks to promote pupils' spiritual, moral, social and cultural development.

STRENGTH						WEAKNESS
1	2	3	4	5	6	7

School: Audit year:

Rating for spiritual, moral, social and cultural development

```
STRENGTH                                          WEAKNESS
   1         2         3         4         5         6         7
7 points  6 points  5 points  4 points  3 points  2 points  1 point
```
☐ ☐ ☐ ☐ ☐ ☐ ☐ NUMBER OF RESPONSES

☐ ☐ ☐ ☐ ☐ ☐ ☐ POINTS PER LEVEL

TOTAL SCORE FOR THIS SECTION OF THE AUDIT ☐

TARGET | 77 |

Principal strengths as identified by the audit

Principal weaknesses as identified by the audit

Action points for the next development plan

The materials in this publication may be photocopied for use only within the purchasing organisation.

47

School: **Audit year:**

Collective worship and assemblies

NOTES

The law requires schools, other than nursery schools and pupil referral units, to provide a daily act of collective worship. Taken over a term, the majority of such acts of worship should be wholly or mainly of a broadly Christian character.

Much that is identifiably Christian in tone may not necessarily refer to Jesus. However, if the worship consistently fails to relate to Jesus with the spoken or written word, it cannot reasonably be referred to as mainly Christian in character.

Auditors may judge worship not simply in terms of whether it is fulfilling the statutory requirements but also whether it is making a real contribution to the spiritual, moral, social and cultural development of pupils.

In arriving at a judgement about the character and nature of worship in the school, the following general points should be taken into account:

- the words used and/or the activities observed in worship recognise the existence of a deity;
- each act of worship should be considered as a piece, but should be seen alongside the evidence of what has occurred or is planned over a term.

Collective worship should not be judged by the presence or absence of a particular ingredient. It might include, for example, opportunities for prayers, for meditation or reflection upon readings from holy texts or other writings which bring out religious themes, or performances of music, drama or dance.

School: Audit year:

Collective worship and assemblies

Person responsible for this part of the audit:

1. Our school prospectus makes clear to parents their right to withdraw their children from collective worship.

STRENGTH						WEAKNESS
1	2	3	4	5	6	7

2. Our acts of worship are well planned, broadly Christian in character and encourage pupils to explore meaning and purpose, values and beliefs.

STRENGTH						WEAKNESS
1	2	3	4	5	6	7

3. Our acts of worship have a sense of occasion with active pupil participation.

STRENGTH						WEAKNESS
1	2	3	4	5	6	7

4. Parents are frequently invited to attend our assemblies.

STRENGTH						WEAKNESS
1	2	3	4	5	6	7

5. Our assemblies allow pupils time for quiet reflection and include simple prayers.

STRENGTH						WEAKNESS
1	2	3	4	5	6	7

The materials in this publication may be photocopied for use only within the purchasing organisation.

School: Audit year:

Rating for collective worship and assemblies

```
STRENGTH                              WEAKNESS
   1        2        3        4        5        6        7
7 points  6 points  5 points  4 points  3 points  2 points  1 point
```

☐ ☐ ☐ ☐ ☐ ☐ ☐ NUMBER OF RESPONSES

☐ ☐ ☐ ☐ ☐ ☐ ☐ POINTS PER LEVEL

TOTAL SCORE FOR THIS SECTION OF THE AUDIT ☐

TARGET 35

Principal strengths as identified by the audit

[ ]

Principal weaknesses as identified by the audit

[ ]

Action points for the next development plan

[ ]

The materials in this publication may be photocopied for use only within the purchasing organisation.

School: Audit year:

Support, guidance, pupils' welfare and child protection

NOTES

The school's system for the support and guidance of its pupils should be assessed in terms of whether or not it enables them to take full advantage of the educational opportunities offered, and whether it encourages pupils to set high but realistic expectations of themselves.

Effective support and guidance can be assessed by:

- observing the informal relationships which pervade the school;
- examining the planned curriculum;
- assessing whether there is consistent implementation of clear policies;
- identifying the opportunities for informal support which occur during daily routines such as registration, meal times, play and story times.

In this, the class teacher's day-to-day contact plays a crucial role, together with the contribution made by support staff.

The audit should consider how well staff interact with pupils within and outside the classrooms, together with staff accessibility and responsiveness to pupils' needs and the quality of the support they give. The key here is the impact of these matters on pupils' progress, general confidence and ability to cope effectively with everyday life in the school.

Whenever nursery or reception children first enter school, the school's support system should be capable of providing adequate arrangements for their welfare at that special time.

The school must attempt to identify and promote the ways in which it encourages regular attendance, good behaviour and respect for others. It must also have clear strategies with regard to possible harassment and bullying and show consistency across the school with respect to policy and practice concerning child protection measures.

School: **Audit year:**

Support, guidance, pupils' welfare and child protection

Person responsible for this part of the audit:

1. We provide effective support and advice for all our pupils, informed by monitoring of their academic progress, personal development, behaviour and attendance.

STRENGTH						WEAKNESS
1	2	3	4	5	6	7

2. We have effective measures to promote discipline and good behaviour and eliminate oppressive behaviour including all forms of harassment and bullying.

STRENGTH						WEAKNESS
1	2	3	4	5	6	7

3. We have effective child protection procedures in place.

STRENGTH						WEAKNESS
1	2	3	4	5	6	7

4. We are successful in promoting the health, safety and general well-being of our pupils.

STRENGTH						WEAKNESS
1	2	3	4	5	6	7

5. Our pupils with special educational needs are adequately supported within the general class groups.

STRENGTH						WEAKNESS
1	2	3	4	5	6	7

6. We promote regular attendance and good behaviour.

STRENGTH						WEAKNESS
1	2	3	4	5	6	7

7. We give support to those pupils who have had prolonged periods of absence.

STRENGTH						WEAKNESS
1	2	3	4	5	6	7

8. We have effective measures to promote discipline and good behaviour and eliminate oppressive behaviour, including all forms of harassment and bullying.

STRENGTH						WEAKNESS
1	2	3	4	5	6	7

9. The school is attempting to create a climate for good behaviour.

STRENGTH						WEAKNESS
1	2	3	4	5	6	7

10. We deal with specific incidents of misbehaviour effectively.

STRENGTH						WEAKNESS
1	2	3	4	5	6	7

11. The school's approach to child protection helps pupils both to protect themselves and to understand the importance of protecting others.

STRENGTH						WEAKNESS
1	2	3	4	5	6	7

School: **Audit year:**

12. The school's procedures for dealing with instances of possible child abuse are effective.

STRENGTH						WEAKNESS
1	2	3	4	5	6	7

13. Our procedures for liaison with other agencies where children are on the child protection register are effective.

STRENGTH						WEAKNESS
1	2	3	4	5	6	7

14. Staff members are aware of our child protection procedures.

STRENGTH						WEAKNESS
1	2	3	4	5	6	7

15. The school has designated a senior member of staff to have responsibility for coordinating action within the school with respect to child protection matters and for liaising with other agencies.

STRENGTH						WEAKNESS
1	2	3	4	5	6	7

16. We follow ACPC (Area Child Protection Committee) procedures and promptly refer suspected cases of child abuse to the local social services department, or to the police.

STRENGTH						WEAKNESS
1	2	3	4	5	6	7

17. We liaise with other agencies involved in the protection of children, by monitoring the progress of children placed on the child protection register, by submitting reports to the local social services department and case conferences, and by being represented at child protection case conferences.

STRENGTH						WEAKNESS
1	2	3	4	5	6	7

18. We contribute to the prevention of child abuse through teaching which builds awareness of the dangers of abuse, helps children to protect themselves and develops responsible attitudes to adult life and parenthood.

STRENGTH						WEAKNESS
1	2	3	4	5	6	7

19. We take part in training which leads to a greater understanding of the signs and symptoms of child abuse.

STRENGTH						WEAKNESS
1	2	3	4	5	6	7

20. Our staff and other providers are well briefed and sensitive to the agreed approach to health education in the school and to the ages and needs of pupils.

STRENGTH						WEAKNESS
1	2	3	4	5	6	7

The materials in this publication may be photocopied for use only within the purchasing organisation.

School: **Audit year:**

Rating for support, guidance, pupils' welfare and child protection

STRENGTH						WEAKNESS
1	2	3	4	5	6	7
7 points	6 points	5 points	4 points	3 points	2 points	1 point
☐	☐	☐	☐	☐	☐	☐ NUMBER OF RESPONSES
☐	☐	☐	☐	☐	☐	☐ POINTS PER LEVEL

TOTAL SCORE FOR THIS SECTION OF THE AUDIT ☐

TARGET **140**

Principal strengths as identified by the audit

Principal weaknesses as identified by the audit

Action points for the next development plan

School: Audit year:

Health and safety

NOTES

Controlling health and safety risks is an essential element of educational provision. This section of the audit concentrates on the extent to which the school responds to statutory requirements to establish, monitor and review the effectiveness of safe working procedures.

In particular the school must:

- provide safe practice in play areas, classrooms and specialist areas;
- pay attention to health and safety in the preparation and conduct of visits out of school;
- ensure that pupils have knowledge of safe working procedures;
- provide a safe learning environment with due attention paid to the layout, placement of equipment and materials and condition of floors and play areas;
- ensure that equipment is well maintained and in safe condition;
- monitor the general cleanliness of floors and surfaces;
- provide appropriate arrangements for the provision, storage, administration and recording of first-aid equipment.

School: **Audit year:**

Health and safety

Person responsible for this part of the audit:

1. The school has a written statement of health and safety policy.

STRENGTH						WEAKNESS
1	2	3	4	5	6	7

2. The school has a designated member of staff responsible for the implementation of the health and safety policy and the undertaking of regular risk assessment.

STRENGTH						WEAKNESS
1	2	3	4	5	6	7

3. The school has procedures for monitoring and reporting accidents.

STRENGTH						WEAKNESS
1	2	3	4	5	6	7

4. Arrangements have been established for dealing with accidents and emergencies.

STRENGTH						WEAKNESS
1	2	3	4	5	6	7

5. Staff have received health and safety training, such as first aid, the use of specified materials and equipment, and the supervision of outdoor activities.

STRENGTH						WEAKNESS
1	2	3	4	5	6	7

6. The school maintains a record of identified health and safety concerns and the action taken or proposed.

STRENGTH						WEAKNESS
1	2	3	4	5	6	7

7. The school's governing body is fulfilling its legal obligations with respect to environmental issues and health and safety

STRENGTH						WEAKNESS
1	2	3	4	5	6	7

8. The school's site manager/caretaker has a clearly defined role

STRENGTH						WEAKNESS
1	2	3	4	5	6	7

The materials in this publication may be photocopied for use only within the purchasing organisation.

School: Audit year:

Rating for health and safety

```
STRENGTH                                        WEAKNESS
   1        2        3        4        5        6        7
7 points 6 points 5 points 4 points 3 points 2 points 1 point
```

☐ ☐ ☐ ☐ ☐ ☐ ☐ NUMBER OF RESPONSES

☐ ☐ ☐ ☐ ☐ ☐ ☐ POINTS PER LEVEL

TOTAL SCORE FOR THIS SECTION OF THE AUDIT ☐

TARGET 56

Principal strengths as identified by the audit

Principal weaknesses as identified by the audit

Action points for the next development plan

School: **Audit year:**

Partnership with parents and the community

NOTES

The major focus in this section is the extent to which parents support the work of the school and are informed about their children's progress.

A secondary focus is the way in which the school involves the local community and how this affects pupils' attainment, progress and personal development.

The audit attempts to identify ways in which the school encourages a partnership with parents to support their children's learning (for example, by having parents working alongside staff in the classrooms or helping with school visits).

The school must also assess the extent to which its arrangements for reporting to parents complies with the statutory requirements.

The audit enables the school to establish whether there are clear lines of communication and consistency in its relations with parents.

School: Audit year:

Partnership with parents and the community

Person responsible for this part of the audit:

1. The school is encouraging a partnership with parents to support their children's learning.

STRENGTH						WEAKNESS
1	2	3	4	5	6	7

2. The school has clear lines of communication with parents.

STRENGTH						WEAKNESS
1	2	3	4	5	6	7

3. The school's approach to relations with parents is maintained consistently.

STRENGTH						WEAKNESS
1	2	3	4	5	6	7

4. The school does all it can to gain the involvement of all parents.

STRENGTH						WEAKNESS
1	2	3	4	5	6	7

5. The school actively helps parents to understand the curriculum and the teaching.

STRENGTH						WEAKNESS
1	2	3	4	5	6	7

6. We keep our parents informed about their child's progress.

STRENGTH						WEAKNESS
1	2	3	4	5	6	7

7. We have examples of records of regular home–school contacts, such as reading diaries.

STRENGTH						WEAKNESS
1	2	3	4	5	6	7

8. The school's work is enriched by links with the community.

STRENGTH						WEAKNESS
1	2	3	4	5	6	7

9. The format of our annual reports to parents make the arrangements for follow-up discussion clear.

STRENGTH						WEAKNESS
1	2	3	4	5	6	7

10. We encourage the use of reading diaries or logs and other means of maintaining contact with parents over pupils' work.

STRENGTH						WEAKNESS
1	2	3	4	5	6	7

11. We use visitors to the school as a means of contributing to the total curriculum.

STRENGTH						WEAKNESS
1	2	3	4	5	6	7

The materials in this publication may be photocopied for use only within the purchasing organisation.

School: **Audit year:**

12. We have a means of evaluating the effect of visitors contributions on pupils' attainment and progress.

    STRENGTH   WEAKNESS
    1   2   3   4   5   6   7
    ....

13. Our written reports meet the following statutory requirements by showing:

    the pupil's progress in all NC subjects studied;
    progress in all other subjects and activities;
    general progress and an attendance record;
    the pupil's NC assessment results and how these compare with results of pupils of the same age in the school at the end of key stages 1 and 2;
    national comparative information about pupils at the end of key stages 1 and 2
    arrangements to discuss the report with the school.

    STRENGTH   WEAKNESS
    1   2   3   4   5   6   7

School: **Audit year:**

Rating for partnership with parents and the community

STRENGTH						WEAKNESS
1	2	3	4	5	6	7
7 points	6 points	5 points	4 points	3 points	2 points	1 point

☐ ☐ ☐ ☐ ☐ ☐ ☐   NUMBER OF RESPONSES

☐ ☐ ☐ ☐ ☐ ☐ ☐   POINTS PER LEVEL

TOTAL SCORE FOR THIS SECTION OF THE AUDIT ☐

TARGET 91

Principal strengths as identified by the audit

Principal weaknesses as identified by the audit

Action points for the next development plan

The materials in this publication may be photocopied for use only within the purchasing organisation.

School: Audit year:

Leadership and management

NOTES

This important section deals with the effectiveness of governors, the headteacher and staff with management responsibilities who contribute to the quality of education provided by the school and the standards achieved by all of its pupils.

There are three key points. Firstly, the focus must be on impact rather than intentions. Secondly, the judgement is about the quality of leadership and management in the school, rather than a particular style or pattern of leadership. Thirdly, leadership and management should be judged as a whole, taking into account the contributions of the governing body and staff as well as the headteacher.

The governing body has specific statutory responsibilities in the matter of leadership and management. In essence it has the following three main tasks:

- to provide a strategic view of where the school is heading;
- to act as *critical friend* to the school;
- to hold the school to account for the educational standards it achieves and the quality of education it provides.

The headteacher is the professional leader of the school, responsible for the overall direction of its work and for the day-to-day management and organisation. Other staff, such as coordinators and teachers responsible for a nursery class or unit, also have leadership and management functions.

It is essential that, throughout the school's organisation, areas of responsibilities are clearly defined and that there is effective delegation, with staff clear about the role they are required to play in the development and running of the school.

School: Audit year:

Leadership and management

Person responsible for this part of the audit:

1. There is strong leadership in the school, providing clear educational direction for the work of the school.

STRENGTH						WEAKNESS
1	2	3	4	5	6	7

2. Teaching and curriculum development are monitored, evaluated and supported.

STRENGTH						WEAKNESS
1	2	3	4	5	6	7

3. The school has clear aims, values and policies which are reflected through all its work.

STRENGTH						WEAKNESS
1	2	3	4	5	6	7

4. The school, through its development planning, identifies relevant priorities and targets, takes the necessary action, and monitors and evaluates its progress towards them.

STRENGTH						WEAKNESS
1	2	3	4	5	6	7

5. There is a positive ethos, which reflects the school's commitment to high achievement, an effective learning environment, good relationships and equality of opportunity for all pupils.

STRENGTH						WEAKNESS
1	2	3	4	5	6	7

6. The leadership and management produce an effective school: one that promotes and sustains improvement in educational standards achieved and the quality of education provided.

STRENGTH						WEAKNESS
1	2	3	4	5	6	7

7. The governing body is acting as a *critical friend* to the school.

STRENGTH						WEAKNESS
1	2	3	4	5	6	7

8. The governing body holds the school to account for the educational standards it achieves and the quality of education it provides.

STRENGTH						WEAKNESS
1	2	3	4	5	6	7

9. The headteacher has a clear role in the process by which the improvement of quality and standards is sustained.

STRENGTH						WEAKNESS
1	2	3	4	5	6	7

The materials in this publication may be photocopied for use only within the purchasing organisation.

School: **Audit year:**

10. The headteacher has assumed a leadership role in the process by which equality of opportunity for all pupils is achieved.

    STRENGTH   WEAKNESS
    1   2   3   4   5   6   7

11. Management and leadership responsibilities are clearly defined and there is effective delegation.

    STRENGTH   WEAKNESS
    1   2   3   4   5   6   7

12. Staff, including support staff, understand the roles they are encouraged to play in the development and running of the school.

    STRENGTH   WEAKNESS
    1   2   3   4   5   6   7

13. Staff holding responsibility have sufficient expertise and time to carry out their management tasks.

    STRENGTH   WEAKNESS
    1   2   3   4   5   6   7

14. The leadership and management have a significant impact on the work of the school.

    STRENGTH   WEAKNESS
    1   2   3   4   5   6   7

15. The school has a sense of purpose evident in all its work and the involvement of all our staff.

    STRENGTH   WEAKNESS
    1   2   3   4   5   6   7

16. The school appreciates its strengths and is sustaining them.

    STRENGTH   WEAKNESS
    1   2   3   4   5   6   7

17. The school is aware of our weaknesses, both at school and classroom level, and we know how to overcome them.

    STRENGTH   WEAKNESS
    1   2   3   4   5   6   7

18. The school has formalised the process of overcoming weaknesses by including it in its planning process.

    STRENGTH   WEAKNESS
    1   2   3   4   5   6   7

19. We have evidence to show that we insist that all pupils do their best and play a full part in the life of the school.

    STRENGTH   WEAKNESS
    1   2   3   4   5   6   7

20. Staff understand the role of the governing body.

    STRENGTH   WEAKNESS
    1   2   3   4   5   6   7

The materials in this publication may be photocopied for use only within the purchasing organisation.

School: **Audit year:**

21. The proceedings of the governing body enable it to fulfil its responsibilities for strategic planning and the quality of education provided.

STRENGTH						WEAKNESS
1	2	3	4	5	6	7

22. Job descriptions are clear and realistic and staff understand and are committed to them.

STRENGTH						WEAKNESS
1	2	3	4	5	6	7

23. There are sound links between job descriptions, staff appraisal, staff development and the school's decision-making structure.

STRENGTH						WEAKNESS
1	2	3	4	5	6	7

24. The school has a system of regularly monitoring pupils' work.

STRENGTH						WEAKNESS
1	2	3	4	5	6	7

25. The school has agreed and published aims which express high expectations of what pupils can achieve.

STRENGTH						WEAKNESS
1	2	3	4	5	6	7

26. Staff are involved in the formulation of aims, values and policies and of the procedures which arise from them.

STRENGTH						WEAKNESS
1	2	3	4	5	6	7

27. Steps are taken to ensure that teaching and other staff (including staff new to the school) understand the school's aims, values and policies and the procedures which arise from them.

STRENGTH						WEAKNESS
1	2	3	4	5	6	7

28. There is a positive ethos which reflects the school's commitment to high achievement, an effective learning environment, good relationships and equality of opportunity for all pupils.

STRENGTH						WEAKNESS
1	2	3	4	5	6	7

29. The school's prospectus, development plan, and policy documents indicate the main aims and priorities of the school.

STRENGTH						WEAKNESS
1	2	3	4	5	6	7

30. The staff handbook (if available) outlines some of the main policies and procedures associated with the management of the school.

STRENGTH						WEAKNESS
1	2	3	4	5	6	7

The materials in this publication may be photocopied for use only within the purchasing organisation.

School: **Audit year:**

Rating for leadership and management

STRENGTH						WEAKNESS
1	2	3	4	5	6	7
7 points	6 points	5 points	4 points	3 points	2 points	1 point

☐ ☐ ☐ ☐ ☐ ☐ ☐   NUMBER OF RESPONSES

☐ ☐ ☐ ☐ ☐ ☐ ☐   POINTS PER LEVEL

TOTAL SCORE FOR THIS SECTION OF THE AUDIT ☐

TARGET 210

Principal strengths as identified by the audit

Principal weaknesses as identified by the audit

Action points for the next development plan

School: Audit year:

Equal opportunities

NOTES

A key issue to be considered in this section of the audit is the extent to which the school provides equality of access for all pupils to learn and make progress.

An equally important issue is the effectiveness of the school's leadership and management in overseeing the creation and implementation of policies to promote equality of opportunity and high achievement for all pupils.

Evidence in this section should include:

- a scrutiny of the schools' policies;
- staffing structures;
- curricular plans;
- pupils' records;
- discussion with the head, staff and pupils;
- direct observation of actions and relations in and out of classrooms;
- consideration of the educational standards achieved by pupils, including test results;
- consideration of the quality of provision under other sections of this audit.

School: **Audit year:**

Equal opportunities

Person responsible for this part of the audit:

1. The leadership and management strongly promote equal access by all pupils to the full range of opportunities for achievement that the school provides.

STRENGTH						WEAKNESS
1	2	3	4	5	6	7

2. The school reflects equality of opportunity in its aims and objectives, curriculum and organisation, including the grouping of pupils.

STRENGTH						WEAKNESS
1	2	3	4	5	6	7

3. The school monitors pupils' achievements by gender, attainment, background and ethnicity to ensure fairness of treatment.

STRENGTH						WEAKNESS
1	2	3	4	5	6	7

4. We offer relevant role models to all pupils in the distribution of teachers and others within our staffing and management structures, including the allocation of curricular and other responsibilities.

STRENGTH						WEAKNESS
1	2	3	4	5	6	7

5. We provide appropriate support for pupils for whom English is an additional language in order to give them access to the whole curriculum.

STRENGTH						WEAKNESS
1	2	3	4	5	6	7

6. We can produce evidence e.g. school's policies, staffing structures, curricular plans and pupils' records; educational standards achieved by pupils, including examination and other test results etc. indicating our commitment to equal opportunity.

STRENGTH						WEAKNESS
1	2	3	4	5	6	7

The materials in this publication may be photocopied for use only within the purchasing organisation.

School: Audit year:

Rating for equal opportunities

STRENGTH						WEAKNESS
1	2	3	4	5	6	7
7 points	6 points	5 points	4 points	3 points	2 points	1 point

☐ ☐ ☐ ☐ ☐ ☐ ☐ NUMBER OF RESPONSES

☐ ☐ ☐ ☐ ☐ ☐ ☐ POINTS PER LEVEL

TOTAL SCORE FOR THIS SECTION OF THE AUDIT ☐

TARGET 42

Principal strengths as identified by the audit

Principal weaknesses as identified by the audit

Action points for the next development plan

The materials in this publication may be photocopied for use only within the purchasing organisation.

School: Audit year:

Special educational needs

NOTES

Auditors should ensure that the school has regard to the *1994 Code of Practice on the Identification and Assessment of Special Educational Needs* and to the earlier relevant sections of the 1993, 1988 and 1981 Education Acts.

Special educational needs issues permeate every section of this audit. However, this section focuses on the school's fulfilment of its statutory obligations, and on the quality and effectiveness of the general oversight and day-to-day management arrangements shared by the governing body, headteacher and other staff.

It is for the governing body, in cooperation with the headteacher, to determine the school's policy and approach for special educational needs; to set up appropriate staffing and funding arrangements; and to maintain general oversight of special educational needs provision.

Provision for special educational needs should be evident in the school's organisational and curricular structures and the practice in the school.

School: Audit year:

Special educational needs

Person responsible for this part of the audit:

1. The school has a designated *responsible person* for special needs.

STRENGTH						WEAKNESS
1	2	3	4	5	6	7

2. The governing body's annual report informs parents about the success of the special educational needs policy and any significant changes to it; any consultation with the LEA, funding authority or other schools; and the allocation of resources over the previous year to pupils with special educational needs.

STRENGTH						WEAKNESS
1	2	3	4	5	6	7

3. The way that the school allocates responsibilities and the manner in which they are carried out are effective in promoting good and efficient use of special educational needs provision to support pupils' attainment and progress.

STRENGTH						WEAKNESS
1	2	3	4	5	6	7

4. Our provision for special educational needs permeates the school's organisational and curricular structures and the practice in the school.

STRENGTH						WEAKNESS
1	2	3	4	5	6	7

5. All staff work closely with the special educational needs coordinator (SENCO).

STRENGTH						WEAKNESS
1	2	3	4	5	6	7

6. Parents are informed as to who is their main point of contact (normally the SENCO) and who is the school's *responsible person*.

STRENGTH						WEAKNESS
1	2	3	4	5	6	7

7. Our resources, including staffing, are managed effectively and efficiently to support special educational needs policies and pupils' identified needs.

STRENGTH						WEAKNESS
1	2	3	4	5	6	7

8. All staff are sufficiently aware of procedures for identifying, assessing and providing for pupils with special educational needs.

STRENGTH						WEAKNESS
1	2	3	4	5	6	7

9. Pupils' progress is monitored, especially in relation to annual reviews and individual education plans (IEP's).

STRENGTH						WEAKNESS
1	2	3	4	5	6	7

The materials in this publication may be photocopied for use only within the purchasing organisation.

School: **Audit year:**

10. Our assessment, recording and reporting arrangements satisfy statutory requirements.

STRENGTH						WEAKNESS
1	2	3	4	5	6	7

11. Adequate pupil records are being maintained by all staff.

STRENGTH						WEAKNESS
1	2	3	4	5	6	7

12. The use of specialist support from outside agencies is well managed within the school.

STRENGTH						WEAKNESS
1	2	3	4	5	6	7

School: Audit year:

Rating for special educational needs

STRENGTH						WEAKNESS
1	2	3	4	5	6	7
7 points	6 points	5 points	4 points	3 points	2 points	1 point

☐ ☐ ☐ ☐ ☐ ☐ ☐ NUMBER OF RESPONSES

☐ ☐ ☐ ☐ ☐ ☐ ☐ POINTS PER LEVEL

TOTAL SCORE FOR THIS SECTION OF THE AUDIT ☐

TARGET 84

Principal strengths as identified by the audit

Principal weaknesses as identified by the audit

Action points for the next development plan

The materials in this publication may be photocopied for use only within the purchasing organisation.

School: Audit year:

Staffing and professional development

NOTES

This section of the audit focuses in the main on the extent to which the school is staffed to teach the curriculum effectively; whether there is evidence of real teamwork; and whether the school has a sound staff development and in-service training programme. Effective teamwork requires each member of staff to have a clear understanding of his/her own roles and responsibilities and those of others.

The audit team will need to appraise the adequacy of staffing, looking for evidence of the impact of professional development on the quality of teaching. It must evaluate the extent to which the school is staffed and resourced to teach the curriculum effectively, including whether there are any clear features which contribute to, or detract from, quality and standards.

School: Audit year:

Staffing and professional development

Person responsible for this part of the audit:

1. The number, qualifications and experience of teachers and other classroom staff match the demands of the curriculum.

STRENGTH						WEAKNESS
1	2	3	4	5	6	7

2. The staff as a whole have sufficient knowledge and expertise to meet the requirements of the school's curriculum, including areas of learning for the under-fives, religious education and the National Curriculum.

STRENGTH						WEAKNESS
1	2	3	4	5	6	7

3. We have adequate arrangements in place for the induction, appraisal and professional development of staff and these arrangements contribute to the effectiveness of staff.

STRENGTH						WEAKNESS
1	2	3	4	5	6	7

4. All members of staff have a clear understanding of their own roles and responsibilities and those of others.

STRENGTH						WEAKNESS
1	2	3	4	5	6	7

5. We have identified the strengths of the school's staffing resources.

STRENGTH						WEAKNESS
1	2	3	4	5	6	7

6. We have identified the staffing shortfalls which affect the standards achieved and the quality of education provided.

STRENGTH						WEAKNESS
1	2	3	4	5	6	7

7. We attempt to maximise available subject and phase expertise to cover the school curriculum.

STRENGTH						WEAKNESS
1	2	3	4	5	6	7

8. Our teachers have been trained in the phase concerned, for example, nursery education.

STRENGTH						WEAKNESS
1	2	3	4	5	6	7

9. Enough appropriately skilled support staff are available to enable teaching, administration and the day-to-day life of the school to function effectively.

STRENGTH						WEAKNESS
1	2	3	4	5	6	7

The materials in this publication may be photocopied for use only within the purchasing organisation.

School: **Audit year:**

10. Nursery and other classroom assistants work closely with teachers in planning, teaching and recording pupils' progress.

    STRENGTH   WEAKNESS
    1   2   3   4   5   6   7

11. The teaching and support staff working with pupils with special educational needs, or with pupils for whom English is an additional language, are experienced and qualified for such work.

    STRENGTH   WEAKNESS
    1   2   3   4   5   6   7

12. The quality of additional staffing resources, such as therapy or medical support, provided in response to individual statements of special educational need are adequate to meet the need.

    STRENGTH   WEAKNESS
    1   2   3   4   5   6   7

13. We have sound arrangements for inducting all staff new to the school, and for those assuming new roles and responsibilities.

    STRENGTH   WEAKNESS
    1   2   3   4   5   6   7

14. The induction arrangements for newly qualified teaching staff take account of DfEE guidance.

    STRENGTH   WEAKNESS
    1   2   3   4   5   6   7

15. Our staff development and in-service training programme is effective in motivating staff and in identifying and meeting individual and corporate needs.

    STRENGTH   WEAKNESS
    1   2   3   4   5   6   7

16. Our professional development programme is making a positive contribution to the teaching.

    STRENGTH   WEAKNESS
    1   2   3   4   5   6   7

17. The staff handbook or staff development plan (if produced) gives useful information about the induction, appraisal and professional development of staff.

    STRENGTH   WEAKNESS
    1   2   3   4   5   6   7

18. The quality and extent of the liaison between teachers, and between teachers and nursery assistants (where applicable) is good.

    STRENGTH   WEAKNESS
    1   2   3   4   5   6   7

School: **Audit year:**

Rating for staffing and professional development

STRENGTH						WEAKNESS
1	2	3	4	5	6	7
7 points	6 points	5 points	4 points	3 points	2 points	1 point

☐ ☐ ☐ ☐ ☐ ☐ ☐ NUMBER OF RESPONSES

☐ ☐ ☐ ☐ ☐ ☐ ☐ POINTS PER LEVEL

TOTAL SCORE FOR THIS SECTION OF THE AUDIT ☐

TARGET 126

Principal strengths as identified by the audit

Principal weaknesses as identified by the audit

Action points for the next development plan

The materials in this publication may be photocopied for use only within the purchasing organisation.

School: **Audit year:**

Accommodation

NOTES

There are no statutory standards for assessing the adequacy of accommodation. However the size of a teaching space has an impact upon the quality of the learning environment, as do the equipment, facilities and services provided.

School: Audit year:

Accommodation

Person responsible for this part of the audit:

1. Our accommodation is adequate for the numbers on roll and ages of pupils as well as the range of curriculum activities, including outdoor areas and space for large equipment and practical work for under-fives and other pupils.

STRENGTH						WEAKNESS
1	2	3	4	5	6	7

2. The school makes good use of the accommodation available, allowing the curriculum to be taught effectively.

STRENGTH						WEAKNESS
1	2	3	4	5	6	7

3. We have identified the strengths of the school's accommodation.

STRENGTH						WEAKNESS
1	2	3	4	5	6	7

4. We have identified the accommodation shortfalls which affect the standards achieved and the quality of education provided.

STRENGTH						WEAKNESS
1	2	3	4	5	6	7

5. Our accommodation, including outdoor areas, provide a stimulating and well-maintained learning environment.

STRENGTH						WEAKNESS
1	2	3	4	5	6	7

6. Our accommodation, furniture and acoustics enable pupils with physical and sensory disabilities to access all areas of the curriculum.

STRENGTH						WEAKNESS
1	2	3	4	5	6	7

7. The school has sufficient facilities and expertise to display work effectively.

STRENGTH						WEAKNESS
1	2	3	4	5	6	7

School: Audit year:

Rating for accommodation

STRENGTH						WEAKNESS
1	2	3	4	5	6	7
7 points	6 points	5 points	4 points	3 points	2 points	1 point

☐ ☐ ☐ ☐ ☐ ☐ ☐   NUMBER OF RESPONSES

☐ ☐ ☐ ☐ ☐ ☐ ☐   POINTS PER LEVEL

TOTAL SCORE FOR THIS SECTION OF THE AUDIT ☐

TARGET 49

Principal strengths as identified by the audit

Principal weaknesses as identified by the audit

Action points for the next development plan

School: Audit year:

Learning resources

NOTES

Learning resources must be assessed as to their appropriateness in range, quality, quantity and effective deployment. Good quality resources reflect the interests of pupils and present gender and cultural diversity in a positive way.

This section of the audit focuses upon the range, quality, type and accessibility of resources being utilised by the school, including books, materials and equipment.

School: **Audit year:**

Learning resources

Person responsible for this part of the audit:

1. Our learning resources are appropriate in range, quality and quantity and are deployed well.

STRENGTH						WEAKNESS
1	2	3	4	5	6	7

2. The library is adequately resourced enabling it to play a central role in supporting learning.

STRENGTH						WEAKNESS
1	2	3	4	5	6	7

3. Our provision of information technology resources across the curriculum adequately supports learning.

STRENGTH						WEAKNESS
1	2	3	4	5	6	7

4. The school effectively utilises resources beyond the school, including museums, galleries and field centres, to enrich the curriculum.

STRENGTH						WEAKNESS
1	2	3	4	5	6	7

5. The school/class libraries, reading materials, textbooks, resource collections, outdoor play equipment, museum/art loans, natural and historical artefacts, are having beneficial effects on the breadth of the curriculum and the school's ability to address the needs of all pupils.

STRENGTH						WEAKNESS
1	2	3	4	5	6	7

6. We include the use of educational visits and school visitors as a valuable resource.

STRENGTH						WEAKNESS
1	2	3	4	5	6	7

School: Audit year:

Rating for learning resources

STRENGTH						WEAKNESS
1	2	3	4	5	6	7
7 points	6 points	5 points	4 points	3 points	2 points	1 point

☐ ☐ ☐ ☐ ☐ ☐ ☐ NUMBER OF RESPONSES

☐ ☐ ☐ ☐ ☐ ☐ ☐ POINTS PER LEVEL

TOTAL SCORE FOR THIS SECTION OF THE AUDIT ☐

TARGET 42

Principal strengths as identified by the audit

Principal weaknesses as identified by the audit

Action points for the next development plan

The materials in this publication may be photocopied for use only within the purchasing organisation.

School: **Audit year:**

School libraries

NOTES

This section attempts to identify the quantity and quality of books in the school supporting the curriculum and suitable for the age range and reading competence of pupils, together with the way in which library facilities are organised and utilised by pupils and staff.

The audit team will need to sample the range of the library stock in order to assess:

- whether there are enough books to support the curriculum;
- if the stock is suitable for the age range of pupils and their competence as readers;
- whether the books reflect and expand the cultural background, interests and learning of the children.

A consideration of the ratio of books to pupils is an important issue with regard to adequacy of provision. Equally important is an examination of the actual use of books in both the main library and, where applicable, classroom libraries; and the match of these to pupils' needs.

The auditors should observe pupils using the library provision in a range of contexts and check that stocks are accessible at the time when the pupils need to use them.

The confidence with which pupils find the book/s they need should also be noted.

School: Audit year:

School libraries

Person responsible for this part of the audit:

1. There are enough books in the school library stock to support the curriculum.

STRENGTH						WEAKNESS
1	2	3	4	5	6	7

2. The books are suitable for the age range of pupils and their competence as readers.

STRENGTH						WEAKNESS
1	2	3	4	5	6	7

3. The range of books reflects and expands the cultural backgrounds, interests, and learning of the pupils.

STRENGTH						WEAKNESS
1	2	3	4	5	6	7

4. Our pupils are taught library skills and the use of the library is encouraged in lessons.

STRENGTH						WEAKNESS
1	2	3	4	5	6	7

5. Our pupils are using the library provision for a range of contexts.

STRENGTH						WEAKNESS
1	2	3	4	5	6	7

6. The library stocks are accessible when the children need to use them.

STRENGTH						WEAKNESS
1	2	3	4	5	6	7

7. Our pupils are confident in finding what they need and selecting books and other resources.

STRENGTH						WEAKNESS
1	2	3	4	5	6	7

8. The way in which our library is organised helps pupils to make the most effective use of it.

STRENGTH						WEAKNESS
1	2	3	4	5	6	7

The materials in this publication may be photocopied for use only within the purchasing organisation.

School: **Audit year:**

Rating for school libraries

STRENGTH						WEAKNESS	
1	2	3	4	5	6	7	
7 points	6 points	5 points	4 points	3 points	2 points	1 point	
☐	☐	☐	☐	☐	☐	☐	NUMBER OF RESPONSES
☐	☐	☐	☐	☐	☐	☐	POINTS PER LEVEL

TOTAL SCORE FOR THIS SECTION OF THE AUDIT ☐

TARGET 56

Principal strengths as identified by the audit

[ ]

Principal weaknesses as identified by the audit

[ ]

Action points for the next development plan

[ ]

School: Audit year:

The efficiency of the school

NOTES

Under this heading the auditors can assess the efficiency with which the resources made available to the school are managed, including the use made of specific grants and the allocation and use of funds for pupils with special educational needs.

Close consideration should be given to budgetary planning, especially where the school has a significant surplus or significant deficit, and also to evidence of the fact that the school is planning ahead.

The following key issues need to be addressed under this section of the audit:

- Are educational developments supported through careful financial planning?
- Is there efficient financial control and school administration?
- Is effective use being made of staff, accommodation and learning resources?
- Does the school provide value for money in terms of educational standards achieved and the quality of education provided in relation to its context and income?

School: **Audit year:**

The efficiency of the school

Person responsible for this part of the audit:

1. We undertake educational developments which are supported through careful financial planning.

STRENGTH						WEAKNESS
1	2	3	4	5	6	7

2. We are making effective use of staff, accommodation and learning resources.

STRENGTH						WEAKNESS
1	2	3	4	5	6	7

3. There is efficient financial control and school administration.

STRENGTH						WEAKNESS
1	2	3	4	5	6	7

4. The school is providing value for money in terms of the educational standards achieved and quality of education provided in relation to its context and income.

STRENGTH						WEAKNESS
1	2	3	4	5	6	7

5. We make good use of all our available resources to achieve the best possible outcomes for all our pupils – thereby providing value for money in terms of the educational standards achieved and quality of education provided.

STRENGTH						WEAKNESS
1	2	3	4	5	6	7

6. The school can account for the expenditure to which it is committed.

STRENGTH						WEAKNESS
1	2	3	4	5	6	7

7. We budget systematically for new expenditure.

STRENGTH						WEAKNESS
1	2	3	4	5	6	7

8. We regularly analyse the use of resources.

STRENGTH						WEAKNESS
1	2	3	4	5	6	7

9. We have adequate reasons for a significant surplus or deficit on the current budget.

STRENGTH						WEAKNESS
1	2	3	4	5	6	7

10. We are clear as to the actions are we proposing to take with respect to the budget surplus/deficit.

STRENGTH						WEAKNESS
1	2	3	4	5	6	7

11. We have our own costs per pupil figures calculated.

STRENGTH						WEAKNESS
1	2	3	4	5	6	7

School: **Audit year:**

12. We focus effectively on improving educational outcomes and relating expenditure to this end in school development planning.

STRENGTH						WEAKNESS
1	2	3	4	5	6	7

13. We can provide evidence of our forward planning and we have prepared outline planning for the next two years, based on sound projections.

STRENGTH						WEAKNESS
1	2	3	4	5	6	7

14. The governing body is fulfilling its strategic responsibility for planning the use of resources.

STRENGTH						WEAKNESS
1	2	3	4	5	6	7

15. We involve all staff with management responsibility in financial planning.

STRENGTH						WEAKNESS
1	2	3	4	5	6	7

16. We are keeping staff informed concerning financial planning issues.

STRENGTH						WEAKNESS
1	2	3	4	5	6	7

17. We have efficient financial control and school administration.

STRENGTH						WEAKNESS
1	2	3	4	5	6	7

18. The main recommendations of the last audit report have been acted upon.

STRENGTH						WEAKNESS
1	2	3	4	5	6	7

19. The headteacher and governing body receive adequate information concerning school finances.

STRENGTH						WEAKNESS
1	2	3	4	5	6	7

20. Our administrative procedures are unobtrusive, resulting in efficient day-to-day organisation and the capacity to respond to the unforeseen event.

STRENGTH						WEAKNESS
1	2	3	4	5	6	7

The materials in this publication may be photocopied for use only within the purchasing organisation.

School: **Audit year:**

Rating for the efficiency of the school

STRENGTH						WEAKNESS
1	2	3	4	5	6	7
7 points	6 points	5 points	4 points	3 points	2 points	1 point

☐ ☐ ☐ ☐ ☐ ☐ ☐ NUMBER OF RESPONSES

☐ ☐ ☐ ☐ ☐ ☐ ☐ POINTS PER LEVEL

TOTAL SCORE FOR THIS SECTION OF THE AUDIT ☐

TARGET 140

Principal strengths as identified by the audit

Principal weaknesses as identified by the audit

Action points for the next development plan

School: Audit year:

Financial administration: additional points

NOTES

This section of the school audit is concerned specifically with the nature of the financial checks and balances operating within the school to maintain financial stability and allowing it to plan and move forward.

A wide range of issues are considered including the effectiveness of financial controls, the relationship between the budget and the identified educational objectives and the insurance cover held by the school.

School: **Audit year:**

Financial administration: additional points

Person responsible for this part of the audit:

1. The responsibilities of the governing body, its committees, the headteacher and staff are clearly defined and the limits of delegated authority are well established.

    STRENGTH   WEAKNESS
    1   2   3   4   5   6   7

2. The school budget reflects our prioritised educational objectives.

    STRENGTH   WEAKNESS
    1   2   3   4   5   6   7

3. The budget is subject to regular and effective monitoring.

    STRENGTH   WEAKNESS
    1   2   3   4   5   6   7

4. We ensure that our purchasing arrangements achieve the best value for money.

    STRENGTH   WEAKNESS
    1   2   3   4   5   6   7

5. The school has sound internal financial controls in place to ensure the reliability and accuracy of its financial transactions.

    STRENGTH   WEAKNESS
    1   2   3   4   5   6   7

6. The school is adequately insured against exposure to risks.

    STRENGTH   WEAKNESS
    1   2   3   4   5   6   7

7. Where school computers are used for administrative purposes, this is registered under the Data Protection Act 1984 and all data is protected against loss.

    STRENGTH   WEAKNESS
    1   2   3   4   5   6   7

8. We have established efficient procedures for the administration of personnel matters including payroll.

    STRENGTH   WEAKNESS
    1   2   3   4   5   6   7

9. Stocks, stores and other assets are recorded, and adequately safeguarded against loss or theft.

    STRENGTH   WEAKNESS
    1   2   3   4   5   6   7

School: **Audit year:**

10. All income due to the school is clearly identified and all collections are receipted, recorded and banked promptly.

    STRENGTH   WEAKNESS
    1   2   3   4   5   6   7
    ....

11. The school properly controls the operation of bank accounts and reconciles bank balances with the accounting records.

    STRENGTH   WEAKNESS
    1   2   3   4   5   6   7
    ....

12. We carefully control the use of petty cash.

    STRENGTH   WEAKNESS
    1   2   3   4   5   6   7
    ....

13. The school administers its voluntary funds as rigorously as public funds.

    STRENGTH   WEAKNESS
    1   2   3   4   5   6   7

School: Audit year:

Rating for financial administration

STRENGTH						WEAKNESS
1	2	3	4	5	6	7
7 points	6 points	5 points	4 points	3 points	2 points	1 point

☐ ☐ ☐ ☐ ☐ ☐ ☐   NUMBER OF RESPONSES

☐ ☐ ☐ ☐ ☐ ☐ ☐   POINTS PER LEVEL

TOTAL SCORE FOR THIS SECTION OF THE AUDIT ☐

TARGET 91

Principal strengths as identified by the audit

Principal weaknesses as identified by the audit

Action points for the next development plan

School: Audit year:

Evaluating value for money and efficiency

NOTES

In judging whether the school is providing value for money the audit team must relate the educational standards achieved, and the quality of education being provided by the school, to its income. Such judgements should be based on the team's conclusions concerning the following issues:

Contextual factors

How are the socio-economic circumstances of the school's pupils supporting or hindering their educational progress? Place that within the range *very favourable – very unfavourable*.

Where can the attainments of the intake on entry be placed within the range *very high – very low*?

Against these contextual issues the following outcomes must be identified and compared:

Outcomes
- pupils' attainments in relation to national averages or expectations as assessed by the range *excellent – very poor*.
- pupils' progress within the range *excellent – very poor*.
- pupils' attitudes, behaviour and personal development within the range *excellent – very poor*.

Provision

The quality of education provided by the school, particularly the teaching, as assessed by the range *excellent – very poor*.

Expenditure

The unit cost of the school should be calculated. How does this compare with other schools of similar type within the range *very low – very high*.

Value for money judgement

It is against these issues of contextual factors, outcomes, provision and expenditure that an objective judgement concerning value for money provided by the school can be arrived at and placed within the range *excellent – very poor*.

School: **Audit year:**

Evaluating value for money and efficiency

Person responsible for this part of the audit:

The socio-economic circumstances of our pupils are

VERY FAVOURABLE					VERY UNFAVOURABLE	
1	2	3	4	5	6	7

Evidence?

The attainment of the intake on entry is

VERY HIGH					VERY LOW	
1	2	3	4	5	6	7

Evidence?

School: **Audit year:**

Pupils' attainment in relation to national averages or expectations is

EXCELLENT						VERY POOR
1	2	3	4	5	6	7

Evidence?

Pupils' progress is

VERY POOR						EXCELLENT
1	2	3	4	5	6	7

Evidence?

School: Audit year:

Your school profile

NOTES

The final section of this audit provides an overall profile of the school, using the data gathered during the full audit.

As stated in the Introduction (p. 7), the principal objective of the audit is *to provide the school with a complete assessment of its current stage of development, as measured against those issues which must be addressed by OFSTED inspectors during inspection.*

By plotting the school's scores against a profile generated by assuming a maximum score for each section of the audit, a graphical representation of the school's current stage of development can be obtained, indicating relative strengths and weaknesses.

This data, together with those action points identified by the audit team, can then be incorporated directly into a management/development plan.

School: Audit year:

Your school profile

A: Standard profile

B: Your school profile

	Section	A	B
National comparisons and evidence of pupil progress	1	70	
Attitudes, behaviour and personal development	2	182	
Attendance	3	21	
Teaching	4	175	
Curriculum planning – general issues	5	112	
Curriculum planning – medium-term	6	56	
Curriculum planning – short-term	7	91	
The school development plan	8	119	
Professional issues	9	28	
Curriculum	10	98	
Assessment, recording and reporting	11	112	
Health education	12	49	
Spiritual, moral, social and cultural development	13	77	
Collective worship and assemblies	14	35	
Support, guidance, pupils' welfare and child protection	15	140	
Health and safety	16	56	
Partnership with parents and the community	17	91	
Leadership and management	18	210	
Equal opportunities	19	42	
Special educational needs	20	84	
Staffing and professional development	21	126	
Accommodation	22	49	
Learning resources	23	42	
School libraries	24	56	
The efficiency of the school	25	140	
Financial administration: additional points	26	91	

The materials in this publication may be photocopied for use only within the purchasing organisation.

School: Audit year:

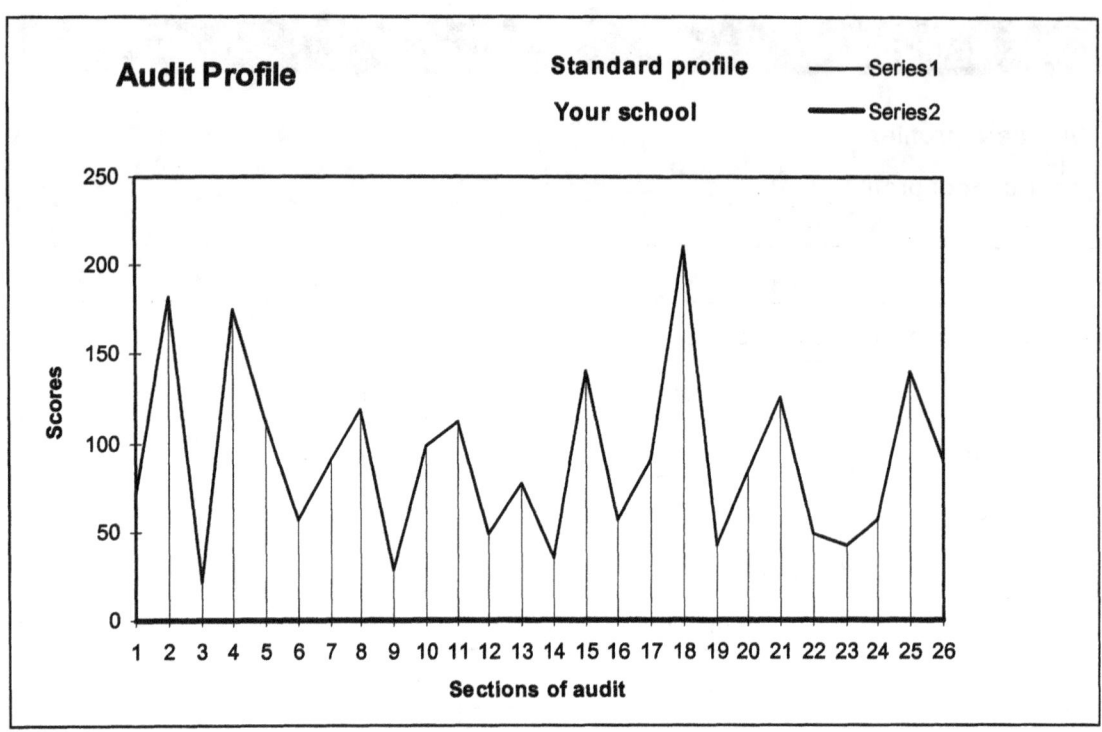

Excel disk version available on request from Cipher Publications, 45 The Green, Lund, Driffield, East Yorks. YO25 9TE.

KEY

1 National comparisons and evidence of pupil progress
2 Attitudes, behaviour and personal development
3 Attendance
4 Teaching
5 Curriculum planning – general issues
6 Curriculum planning – medium-term
7 Curriculum planning – short-term
8 The school development plan
9 Professional issues
10 Curriculum
11 Assessment, recording and reporting
12 Health education
13 Spiritual, moral, social and cultural development
14 Collective worship and assemblies
15 Support, guidance, pupils' welfare and child protection
16 Health and safety
17 Partnership with parents and the community
18 Leadership and management
19 Equal opportunities
20 Special educational needs
21 Staffing and professional development
22 Accommodation
23 Learning resources
24 School libraries
25 The efficiency of the school
26 Financial administration

School: **Audit year:**

When the Registered Inspector calls

NOTES

An OFSTED inspection team requires certain information in advance in order to understand the way in which the school operates. In the main, this is limited to what a school would normally be expected to have in place. Inspectors will need to see:

- the headteacher's Form and Statement;
- the school prospectus;
- the school development plan (or equivalent);
- minutes of governing body meetings for the last 12 months;
- the last annual report to parents and governors;
- the staff handbook (if one is available);
- curriculum policies, plans and guidelines for schemes of work already in existence;
- plan of the school;
- teaching time-tables for the week of the inspection;
- other policy documents which are available in the school.

During the inspection the team will require access to other material needed to follow up particular enquiries, such as:

- samples of pupils' work (from the previous year if the inspection is early in the school year);
- pupils' records and reports;
- documents for pupils having special educational needs (IEPs and SEN Statements);
- teachers' planning and assessment documents, including guidelines or schemes of work not provided earlier;
- attendance registers.

Notes

Notes

Notes

For Product Safety Concerns and Information please contact our EU
representative GPSR@taylorandfrancis.com
Taylor & Francis Verlag GmbH, Kaufingerstraße 24, 80331 München, Germany

www.ingramcontent.com/pod-product-compliance
Lightning Source LLC
Chambersburg PA
CBHW080833010526
44112CB00015B/2504